Handbook for Christian EFL Teachers

Christian Teacher-Preparation Programs,
Overseas Teaching Opportunities,
Instructional Materials and Resources

Lonna J. Dickerson
Dianne F. Dow

Institute for Cross-Cultural Training
Billy Graham Center
Wheaton College
Wheaton, IL

A • B G C • M O N O G R A P H

©1997 by Billy Graham Center

Published by Berry Publishing Services, Inc.
701 Main Street
Evanston, IL 60202-1701

and

Institute for Cross Cultural Studies
Billy Graham Center
Wheaton College
Wheaton, IL 60187-5593

Printed in the United States of America

Billy Graham Center ISBN 1-879089-25-4

Berry Publishing Services, Inc. ISBN 0-9635856-1-4

Project Manager: *Tonya Eichelberger*
Sales Representative: *Jerry Proctor*
Art Director: *April Love-Bailey*
Back Cover Copy: *David Broersma*

For information about mission, seminary and college information handbooks available from Berry Publishing Services, Inc., visit our Website: http://www.berrypub.com

For information about the Billy Graham Center and BGC publications, visit our Website: http://www.wheaton.edu/bgc/bgc.htm

Preface

Are you a missionary, missionary appointee, or Christian tentmaker? Is your objective to have an English-teaching ministry? If so, perhaps you are asking questions such as these:

- What kind of professional preparation do I need in order to teach overseas?

- Where can I find teacher-preparation courses and/or degree programs in the field? Which Christian colleges and universities offer appropriate instruction?

- What overseas teaching opportunities are there for Christian tentmakers? What opportunities exist with mission agencies and other Christian organizations?

- What teacher-training books and other materials are available to help me learn how to teach English? Where can they be purchased?

- What types of materials are available to use with learners of English? What are the criteria for selecting materials? Where can I buy them?

- What other resources (journals, professional organizations, Internet information, clearinghouses, networking opportunities) can I draw upon?

The Handbook for Christian EFL Teachers offers straightforward answers to the above questions. While this volume is primarily for persons whose teaching ministry is overseas, it also contains a great deal |of useful information for those who teach in North America. Each chapter examines practical issues that Christians must address when planning for an effective EFL-teaching ministry.

If this is the first book you have read about teaching English to speakers of other languages, we encourage you to begin with the list of acronyms and the introductory pages of each chapter. This will give you an overview of some key areas in which you may need to make decisions. However, if you are already an ESL/EFL teacher, or if you have taken course work in TESL/TEFL, you may wish to begin your reading with the sections that are most relevant to your immediate needs.

Although we have worked carefully to be accurate in our listings of Christian colleges and universities as well as Christian agencies involved in overseas EFL teaching, we welcome your corrections and additions. Likewise, our goal has been to list professional resources and classroom materials that are up-to-date and particularly relevant in overseas contexts. We solicit your comments on these listings, and invite your suggestions of other useful publications and resources that we can include in the next edition.

We would like to express our appreciation to those who have helped and encouraged us in the preparation of this handbook. We are especially indebted to our husbands, Wayne Dickerson and Bruce Dow, for their careful and candid critique of the manuscript in its various stages and for their unconditional support from the beginning through the completion of this project. We would also like to thank our TESL/TEFL colleagues, David Broersma, Carolyn Dirksen, Laura Hahn, Cheri Pierson, and Alan Seaman for their insightful comments and suggestions, and we are grateful to Watha Shore for her careful tabulating of the survey data.

Three individuals from the Billy Graham Center, Wheaton College, also deserve our thanks. When we first approached Jim Kraakevik, the former Director, he encouraged us to pursue this project and offered many helpful suggestions for making our dream a reality. More recently, Ken Gill, the current Acting Director, has continued to support us with encouragement and sound advice. In addition, Dotsey Welliver, the BGC Editorial Coordinator, has offered invaluable assistance in editing the manuscript.

Finally, we wish to thank Berry Publishing Services, Inc., for their role in publishing this handbook and making sure it reaches those who might find it of value. In particular, we appreciate the direction and assistance of the publisher, Bill Berry, and his associates Jerry Proctor, Rob Ambrose, Dala Bruemmer, Leona Pitej, April Love-Bailey, and Tonya Eichelberger.

Contents

Acronyms

The following acronyms, used throughout this text, occur frequently in publications that deal with teaching English to those who are native speakers of other languages.

EFL	English as a foreign language: English taught/learned in countries where English is not commonly used as (1) the medium of general communication and (2) the medium of academic instruction. For example, those who teach English in Russia, Turkey, and China teach English as a foreign language.
ESL	English as a second language: English taught/learned in an English-speaking country such as the United States and a large part of Canada. The learners are often (1) immigrants or refugees who plan to remain in the country or (2) students who may return to their native countries after a period of study. Although we use the term "second" language, English may be the learners' third, fourth, or even tenth language.

Some authors and practitioners in the field blur the contrast between ESL and EFL. North Americans often use ESL as a generic acronym to refer to teaching English to native speakers of other languages regardless of the country or environment in which instruction takes place; in other parts of the world, the term EFL is preferred. In this text, we will keep the two terms distinct.

ELT	English language teaching or English language training: Used most often outside North America, a generic term for ESL/EFL teaching/learning.
ESOL	English for speakers of other languages: Often used interchangeably with ESL or as a generic term for ESL/EFL.
EAP	English for academic purposes: The teaching or learning of the varieties of English used in academic work (e.g., English for Biblical and Theological Studies).
ESP	English for specific purposes: The teaching or learning of the varieties of English used for specific job-related tasks or skills (e.g., Business English).
TEFL	Teaching English as a foreign language: Teacher preparation degree or course work for EFL teachers.
TESL	Teaching English as a second language: Teacher preparation degree or course work for ESL teachers. Some authors and practitioners in the field blur the distinction between TESL and TEFL.
TESOL	Teaching English to speakers of other languages: Used interchangeably with TESL or as a generic term for TESL/TEFL.
TESOL	Teachers of English to Speakers of Other Languages: The name of the international association of ESL/EFL teachers, materials writers, teacher trainers, curriculum developers, researchers, and program administrators. Based in Washington, D.C., with affiliates in many other countries.
IATEFL	International Association of Teachers of English as a Foreign Language: Similar in membership and purpose to TESOL, an organization for ESL/EFL specialists. Based in the United Kingdom with branches in other countries.
RSA	Royal Society of Arts: The developer of a number of teacher-training courses and examinations in the United Kingdom and elsewhere.
USCES	University of Cambridge Local Examinations Syndicate: The developer of a number of teacher-training courses and examinations in the United Kingdom and elsewhere.
CTEFLA	Certificate in the Teaching of English as a Foreign Language to Adults: Another name for the RSA/USCES teacher training course and examination.
TOEFL	Test of English as a Foreign Language: A language proficiency test for internationals making application to colleges and universities in English-speaking countries. Administered in locations around the world, including the United States.

1. Four Key Questions

What is the role of English in the world?

English is truly a world language. Although estimates vary, as many as one billion people speak English as a native language or use it as a second or foreign language. Crystal (1987, p. 358) notes that more than 60 countries claim English as the official or semi-official language, and another 20 accord it a prominent position. He says that approximately three-fourths of the world's mail is written in English and more than two-thirds of the world's scientists publish in English. Indeed, this is the primary language of international business and academic conferences, books, journals, newspapers, education, science, technology, medicine, sports, music, advertising, politics, commerce, and finance, as well as international mission organizations.

EFL learners differ in their reasons for wanting to learn English. From Japan to Venezuela to Bulgaria, many thousands of university students are eager to improve their English skills in order to qualify for admission to colleges and universities in English-speaking countries. In Mexico City, Taipei, and Nairobi, young adults with a facile command of conversational English compete for the more highly paid positions in business, science, and technology. An increasing number of Christians in Eastern Europe and the former Soviet Union require English in order to read biblical and theological books and materials not available in their native languages or to attend seminaries and Bible schools where English is the medium of instruction. Christian missionaries from Korea, Europe, and South America must have sufficient English proficiency to communicate with their multinational colleagues.

What is the need for EFL teachers?

As the worldwide demand for English instruction has increased each year, the need for EFL teachers has also expanded dramatically. Consequently, Christian tentmakers and missionaries—if they are also well-qualified EFL teachers—have access to a wide range of instructional opportunities. These include teaching in educational institutions (universities, colleges, elementary and secondary schools, including schools for missionary children, language institutes, business institutes, seminaries, Bible schools); teaching in English-language camps for adults and/or children; teaching for government agencies, overseas corporations, or private U.S. companies with offices abroad; teaching in programs sponsored by Christian agencies or local churches; and private tutoring. Because of this unprecedented demand for EFL instruction, overseas openings exist for several thousand Christians who are also qualified EFL teachers. Furthermore, we anticipate a steady growth in demand for those with professional preparation.

Although many teachers find openings in existing programs, others must recruit students, design a curriculum, select textbooks, and train teachers. These tasks may sound daunting for those who lack background in this field of instruction. However, a variety of teacher-preparation programs as well as a large number of publications and other resources are available to help those who wish to become effective EFL tutors, classroom teachers, administrators, materials writers, and teacher trainers. Many of those programs and resources are listed in this volume.

Who can become an effective EFL teacher?

When they consider teaching English overseas, Christians often divide into one of two groups. Some think, "I'm a native speaker of English (or a very good non-native speaker); therefore, I am well prepared to teach English. I'll just pick up a textbook, start teaching, and everything will go fine." Others see their innate abilities very differently, thinking, "My educational background and experience are in another field. Besides, English grammar scares me to death, and I know nothing about how to teach English to those who do not already speak the language." Without adequate training, neither of these groups of prospective teachers is likely to be successful at teaching EFL. With appropriate preparation, however, most individuals who are willing to work hard and who enjoy teaching, especially in cross-cultural contexts, can become competent EFL teachers.

Although native English speakers are frequently in higher demand for teaching listening and speaking skills, non-native speakers of English with advanced language skills can also be very good EFL professionals. If teachers in this latter group are working in their home countries, they generally have an advantage because they speak the same language as their students, and they know the culture from an insider's point of view. Furthermore, age and background are no barriers to a satisfying EFL-teaching experience. Teachers can be college students, recent graduates, middle-aged individuals, or retirees; they can be pastors and missionaries, or they can be businessmen and businesswomen, laypersons, elementary and secondary school teachers, and university professors. In short, effective EFL teachers can be native or non-native speakers of English, and they can come from almost any age group and from any line of work.

How can EFL teaching be a tool for Christian ministry?

Teaching English is one of the fastest-growing areas of ministry for Christians working overseas. Thousands of individuals, as well as dozens of mission agencies, now view EFL teaching as a vehicle for modeling Christian love among people who otherwise might never meet a Christian. Baurain (1992, p. 167) points out that, "Students are likely to be impressed by excellence of teaching, a commitment to the task, a caring attitude, an 'as unto the Lord' work ethic, and clear moral standards." Relationships begun initially in the classroom often carry over into out-of-class opportunities to deepen friendships, demonstrate a Christian lifestyle, and share the Good News.

Relationships with foreign nationals, however, need not start inside the classroom. Almost everywhere in the world, those eager to improve their language skills seek out native English speakers for informal conversation practice. Frequently, these language learners are the country's elite—business people, public officials, and educators, as well as university students who will be the future leaders of the nation. These eager learners offer EFL teachers extraordinary opportunities not only to develop personal friendships but also to learn about the host culture and language.

Although we often think of EFL teaching as a tool for reaching those who have never heard the gospel message, it is also an instrument for ministering to the needs of Christian nationals. Working through overseas churches and other Christian organizations, mission agencies and parachurch groups are looking for teachers who can offer listening and speaking classes for beginners, conversation groups for intermediate to advanced learners, or perhaps combination Bible study/EFL classes for those who already have a basic command of the language. Especially in Eastern Europe and other locations where few Bible study materials and theological textbooks exist in the national languages, many new converts and mature Christians want a command of English sufficient to understand basic commentaries, theological books, and other biblical resources written in English. This rapidly growing group of believers includes professors and students in seminaries and Bible schools as well as pastors and youth workers in large cities and small villages—many of the key Christian leaders who are reaching their own people with the Good News, discipling new believers, and helping those who have been Christians for many years to grow in their faith. Teaching EFL to these Christian leaders can be the proverbial pebble in the pond, rippling outward to make the gospel known to greater and greater numbers of people.

2. Teacher Preparation

This chapter deals with a number of key questions that students and other newcomers to the profession often ask about teacher preparation: If I speak English, why do I need additional teacher training? How much training do I need? What types of courses are available? Is it possible to get a degree in EFL teaching? Can a Christian school supply me with what I need? After addressing these issues, the chapter presents the findings of our 1996 survey of Christian colleges and universities that offer degrees or course work in TESL/TEFL.

Why do native English speakers (and very competent non-native speakers) need special preparation to teach EFL?

Many people believe the maxim, "If you can speak English, you can teach it." In one sense, this is true. You can serve as a conversation partner for those who already know some English; you can probably correct a host of grammar problems, even if you can't explain why a particular usage is correct; you may be able to help students work through lessons in EFL textbooks; you may even have the expertise to teach literature or composition to university students who are at the advanced level of proficiency. Your ability to speak English will allow you to handle a number of specific teaching responsibilities; however, the *range of tasks* you can perform—and especially the range of tasks that you can perform well—will be severely limited if you lack professional preparation.

In his book, *More Than a Native Speaker: An Introduction for Volunteers Teaching Abroad* (1996, p. 2), Don Snow, a Presbyterian missionary, EFL teacher, and program coordinator, reminds us that knowing how to speak a language is not the same as knowing how to teach that language. He says,

> To a large extent, success in teaching is based on qualities such as diligence, patience, and common sense, which many nonprofessionals possess in abundance, and many volunteer teachers make a significant educational contribution to their host nation in spite of their lack of professional training. However, learning the craft of language teaching by trial and error is a process that can take a long time and involve considerable emotional wear and tear on both volunteer teachers and students.

Echoing Snow's call for professional preparation, Robert Lynes (1996, pp. 4-5) comments, "As well as helping you find work, training can give you the confidence and credibility to stand in front of a group of students [and give] you ideas on what and how to teach. It is not enough just to be a native speaker of English to cope with the problems that come with teaching English....Enthusiasm, imagination, common sense and hard work are all qualities you will need in the classroom, but these alone do not make you a good teacher."

If you are planning to be a tentmaker, you'll find that professional qualifications will enhance your marketability considerably. Those who go overseas with no more than a bachelor's degree—and often even with a master's degree in an unrelated field—may find entry-level positions, but the pay scales tend to be quite low, frequently not enough to live on. In addition, benefits such as housing, health coverage, and travel, as well as the preferred teaching assignments, are sometimes offered only to those with the higher qualifications. Blythe Camenson (1995, pp. 3-4) notes that "the field...has grown enormously in the past two decades. At one time, it was believed that the only qualification necessary to teach English to non-native speakers was to be a native speaker. But...that school of thought has almost vanished. Before the TESOL profession firmly established itself as an important and valid discipline, an individual could venture overseas, finding teaching work along the way to cover travel costs and living expenses. Although such tutoring and part-time teaching situations do still exist in a few locations, they are quickly shrinking, replaced with quality programs touting qualified and experienced ESL/EFL teachers."

There are additional reasons for obtaining appropriate teacher preparation before going overseas. Once you become an EFL teacher, your students and other nationals will quickly assign you to the role of EFL "expert"—the one who knows how to organize a new program and select appropriate teaching materials, the one who excels at teaching all skills and components of English to all possible kinds of learners, the one who is a storehouse of knowledge about the English language. To be the "expert" that you are expected to be requires far more than your good intentions and the ability to speak the language. It requires professional preparation—both course work and practical teaching experience.

In many EFL-teaching situations, professionalism is mandatory for a credible Christian witness. Often desperate to learn English, students who spend their time and their hard-earned money on EFL instruction expect quality teaching that utilizes appropriate methods and materials. In *Evangelical Missions Quarterly* (April 1992, p. 167), Bradley Baurain states, "The central specific issue in making TEFL a viable and fruitful ministry is professionalism. It is not an excuse to be in Poland, nor a cover for slipping into Mongolia; it is the ministry itself." He goes on to cite Mark Dyer, president of International Teams, "...if the teaching is good...the teacher is winning a hearing as a Christian."

How much preparation do I need?

Prospective EFL teachers often ask, "How much preparation will I need to teach English overseas?" The answer depends on your future teaching situation. What will it be like? Will you be teaching formal classes, or will you be tutoring individual students? Will you be teaching alongside experienced EFL teachers, or will you be working alone? Will you need to decide on course content and choose from among the thousands of available textbooks, or will someone else do this for you? Will you need to test prospective students and place them into sections divided according to proficiency level, or will this not be your concern? Which skills (e.g., listening, speaking, reading, writing) and which content areas (e.g., grammar, pronunciation, vocabulary, literature, culture) will you be teaching? Which levels (e.g., beginning, intermediate, advanced) will you be responsible for?

If you are planning to teach English for more than a few weeks as a summer volunteer, it is usually unwise to go overseas without professional preparation. For some assignments, a TEFL short course and some practical teaching experience are sufficient; for others, a certificate or master's degree in TESL/TEFL is the insurance that you need in order to be well prepared.

Can I begin teaching EFL after taking one or two courses?

If you can find a single course geared to your individual needs, this may be a suitable entry-level choice. By taking an introductory course or two, you should acquire a basic foundation for volunteering as a conversation partner, teaching in an already existing program, and tutoring individual students.

College and university courses. Even if they do not offer a degree program in the field, many colleges and universities offer one or more ESL/EFL teacher-preparation courses. When an institution offers only a course or two, these classes are often very practical in emphasis. If you have a choice of courses, make your selection based on the fact that the most crucial areas for a beginning teacher include (1) an overview of TESL/TEFL methods and techniques, including an introduction to teaching content areas such as pronunciation, grammar, vocabulary, and the listening-speaking and reading-writing skills; (2) the evaluation, selection, and adaptation of teaching materials; and (3) supervised practice teaching. If you are taking only one or two courses, you should avoid those that go into depth in only one component or skill area (e.g., English grammar, English phonology, teaching reading, teaching composition) and do not deal with other equally important content areas.

The RSA/Cambridge and Trinity College (UK) programs. Among the several types of certificates, the best known is the RSA/Cambridge Certificate which requires approximately 100-110 clock hours of intensive instruction (Lakin, 1996, pp. 11-12). This course, also known as the RSA CTEFLA or the RSA Preparatory Certificate, is available to native and non-native speakers of English. Offered by more than 240 centers in 40 different countries, it is usually taken as a one-month intensive program, although some EFL training centers offer it for a few hours per week spread out over a number of months. Trinity College London also offers a certificate equivalent to the RSA.[1]

Worldwide, many EFL teaching centers and corporations that employ EFL teachers recognize holders of the RSA/Cambridge Certificate and Trinity Certificate as qualified beginning classroom instructors. These entry-level qualifications, however, do not provide sufficient preparation for higher-level tasks such as administering a program, designing curricula, training teachers, and writing materials.

The RSA/Cambridge Diploma and Trinity College Diploma courses are designed especially for teachers with the certificate and a minimum of two years of classroom experience. These courses are usually ten weeks in length or part-time over several months. They focus on the needs of program administrators, teacher coordinators, and experienced teachers interested in the theoretical as well as the practical aspects of EFL teaching. Diploma courses are frequently offered by the same institutions that offer certificate courses.

Although the knowledge and skill you gain from one or two teacher-preparation courses can launch you into the profession, after a year or more of teaching you may be ready to pursue a more rigorous academic program.

What types of academic programs are available?

Hundreds of educational institutions across North America and elsewhere in the world offer teacher-preparation course work in TESL/TEFL. Discussed below are the types of programs that entry level ESL/EFL teachers select most frequently: the master's degree, the academic certificate, ESL teacher certification for teaching in public schools in the U.S., and the undergraduate major or minor.

Master's degree programs. Most master's degree programs vary from one to two-and-a-half years in length. Some institutions offer a master's in TESL/TEFL (or TESOL) while others offer a master's in Applied Linguistics, English, Education, Intercultural Studies, or Missions with a specialization in TESL/TEFL. Required courses typically include the following areas: introduction to general linguistics; principles of second language acquisition; materials selection and development; teaching methods; supervised practice teaching; intercultural communication or the teaching of culture; language testing; the teaching of grammar, pronunciation, listening, speaking (conversation), reading, and writing. Some programs include courses on psycholinguistics, sociolinguistics, applied linguistics, discourse analysis, and other fields that directly impact EFL teaching and learning.

A person with a master's degree and a minimum of two or three years of teaching experience often has acquired the basic preparation for designing curricula; setting up, administering, and evaluating an EFL program; training classroom teachers; and writing materials.

Academic certificate programs. Often restricted to the graduate level, requirements for an academic certificate vary considerably. Generally, this certificate represents either (1) about one-half to two-thirds of the course work for a master's degree or (2) the same courses as a master's degree, but no thesis is required. Certificate programs frequently have a more practical emphasis than the master's degree.

Some programs offer a master's degree in Applied Linguistics, English, Education, Intercultural Studies or Missions with an accompanying academic certificate in TESL/TEFL. Generally, students can use their master's elective credits toward the certificate so that at most only a few additional courses are required to obtain the academic certificate in addition to the master's degree.

The academic certificate usually provides solid preparation for effective classroom teaching in the U.S. and overseas. In addition, many persons with this qualification should be able to handle the same tasks as those with a master's in TESL/TEFL.

ESL teacher certification for teaching in public schools. This credential is also called teacher endorsement, teacher approval, or a teaching license for elementary and/or secondary education. Although requirements vary, all states offering teacher certification in ESL require a number of education courses as well as a minimum amount of practice teaching. A U.S. master's degree or academic certificate program in TESL/TEFL or TESOL is likely to include most, but perhaps not all, of the required course work for teacher certification in the public schools.

An elementary or secondary ESL teaching certificate, combined with ESL teaching experience, equips individuals particularly well for teaching ESL in schools for missionary children. In addition, these teachers are frequently well prepared to teach EFL to adult learners.

Undergraduate major or minor. A few institutions offer sufficient course work for an undergraduate major or minor in ESL. These programs are often taken by those working toward the teaching certificate for public schools.

Where can I find information about programs?

If you wish to select a teacher-preparation program or course other than one of those listed in Chart I at the end of this chapter, the following references will lead you to a wide range of programs in the United States and elsewhere in the world. Among these are a few Christian colleges and universities with programs listed in Chart I.

Directory of Professional Preparation Programs in TESOL in the United States and Canada, 1995-1997 by Ellen Garshick. Updated approximately every three years, this volume contains basic information about university and college programs: program length, requirements, courses, faculty, tuition and fees, and admission requirements. The most recent directory lists 240 institutions (210 in the United States, 30 in Canada) that offer a total of more than 400 teacher-preparation programs: 36 programs leading to a doctorate, 208 to a master's degree, 67 to a certificate or diploma, 48 to undergraduate programs, and 74 to state teaching endorsement or approval. Available from TESOL Publications (address at the end of Chapter 4).

Directory of TESOL Teacher Training and Applied Linguistics Programs in Australia and New Zealand by ELICOS (English Language Intensive Courses for Overseas Students) Association of Australia. Available from the EA Secretariat, 3 Union Street, Pyrmont, NSW, Australia 2009.

The ELT Guide by Paul Lakin, ed. Published annually, this volume includes some academic programs, especially those in the United Kingdom, but the bulk of the listings are for the hundreds of RSA/Cambridge and Trinity College (UK) courses and other short courses offered worldwide. These include programs for learning to teach General Purpose English as well as courses for teaching English for Specific Purposes (ESP), Business English, and children. Available from *EFL Gazette*, 10 Wrights Lane, London W8 6TA, United Kingdom and from Delta Systems (address at the end of Chapter 4).

Teaching English Abroad by Susan Griffith. This softbound book provides a directory of teacher-training courses, with major emphasis on the RSA/Cambridge and Trinity College (UK) courses. Distributed by Peterson's Guides, Inc., 202 Carnegie Center, Princeton, NJ 08543; published by Vacation Work, 9 Park End Street, Oxford, United Kingdom.

You can also find a large number of programs and courses listed on the World Wide Web (see Chapter 5). Check the listings for *Linguistic Funland, Dave's ESL Cafe, ESOL International*, and *The United States Information Agency (USIA)*.

Should I choose a Christian institution?

We believe that there is no single best choice for Christians. You will need to consider your individual needs and the merits of the programs available to you. Based on informal discussions with a large number of missionaries, missionary candidates, and Christian tentmakers, we find valid reasons for choosing each type of program.

A number of individuals cite the following advantages to choosing a Christian college or university: (1) They prefer a program that integrates EFL teaching with Christian ministry, particularly overseas ministry; (2) they also plan to enroll in classes in related disciplines such as Bible and theology, missions, cross-cultural teaching, and Christian education; (3) they desire to be at an institution where Christian fellowship and networking predominate; and (4) they qualify for financial aid available to missionaries and missionary candidates.

Christians who have studied at secular institutions cite advantages such as these: (1) The cost is sometimes significantly less; (2) a wide variety of teaching assistantships are often available to those at the master's and doctoral levels, especially to those who have had classroom teaching experience; (3) a very large number of programs are available in North America and worldwide; (4) universities may offer a wider selection of TESL/TEFL courses as well as a broad range of related courses in other departments.

Whether you plan to take only one or two courses before teaching EFL or enroll in an academic certificate or master's program, we hope by now that you realize that the saying, "If you speak English, you can also teach it like a pro," is a myth. While being a native speaker or a highly proficient non-native speaker can be very helpful, that alone is not sufficient to make you an effective and confident EFL educator. To be competent at whatever level you plan to teach, you need professional preparation.

Which Christian schools offer degree programs or course work?

This section lists Christian schools in the United States and Canada that offer master's degrees, graduate and undergraduate academic certificates, ESL teacher endorsement, undergraduate majors and/or minors, and individual courses in TESL/TEFL.[2] (See Chart I.) Some of these entries also appear in secular sources such as the books cited in Chapter 5. If you are interested in pursuing course work or a degree at one or more of the following institutions, you should contact the school for additional information. In particular, you should look for answers to questions such as these:

- How large is the faculty? Do many faculty members contribute to instruction, or is the program built around only one or two part-time professors?

- What are the credentials of faculty members? Do they have degrees in TESL/TEFL (or TESOL), applied linguistics, second language acquisition, or a related field with a specialization in TESL/TEFL? Do they have significant practical ESL/EFL teaching experience? Do they have overseas experience?

- Which aspects of TESL/TEFL receive the primary focus? For example, does the program offer a balance of theory and practice with a variety of teaching opportunities? Or does it have a practical emphasis but provides no opportunity for actual teaching? Or is it primarily research-oriented?

- Does the program have the emphasis you want? For example, does it prepare teachers for overseas EFL teaching, or is the emphasis primarily on teaching ESL in North America? Is the focus on adult education, ESL for children, or both?

- What specific courses are offered? If you are planning to take only one or two courses, does the institution offer courses that provide a broad foundation with practical applications, or is each course more narrow in focus and therefore more appropriate as one building block in a larger curriculum?

- How long (semesters or quarters) is the program? Can you start during the summer or spring, or must you begin in the fall?

- What is the cost? Is financial aid available? If so, how much is available and what are the qualifications for aid? Are special fellowships or scholarships available to missionaries and missionary candidates?

---

[1]Before enrolling in the RSA/Cambridge or Trinity College programs, inexperienced teachers with no previous EFL teacher-training course work can take a Pre-Service Certificate in Teaching English.

[2]While our listing of institutions omits a few Christian schools that offer programs or course work in TESL/TEFL, it includes all those that completed our 1996 survey. To locate the qualifying institutions, we contacted more than 150 Christian schools on two separate occasions. No fee was charged for inclusion.

INSTITUTION	Azusa Pacific University Richard Slimbach, Chair, TESOL 901 E. Alosta P.O. Box 7000 Azusa, CA 97102 Tel: (818) 969-3434, x3844	Biola University Herbert C. Purnell, Chair, TESOL and Applied Linguistics 13800 Biola Avenue La Mirada, CA 90639-0001 Tel: (310) 903-4844 E-mail: herb_purnell@peter.biola.edu	Carson-Newman College Ronald G. Midkiff, Dean, International Education Jefferson City, TN 37760 Tel: (423) 471-4447 E-mail: midkiff@cnacc.cn.edu
PROGRAMS			
Master's	M.A., TESOL (36 sem. units); M.A., Education with emphasis in ESL	M.A., TESOL (9 prerequisite sem. units, 32 program sem. units)	M.A., TESL (36–42 sem. hrs)
Certificate	Certificate, TESOL (grad., 21 sem. units)	Certificate, TESOL (grad, 9 prerequisite sem. units, 16 program sem. units)	Certificate, TESL (grad., 12 sem. hrs); Advanced Certificate, TESL (grad., 24 sem. hrs)
Elem./Secondary Teacher Certification			Teacher Licensure for TN
Undergrad. Major	B.A., Global Studies	Minor/Certificate (19 sem. units)	
Undergrad. Minor			
Course Title(s)	Second Language Acquisition; Structures of English; Phonology; Language & Culture; Second Language Pedagogy I & II; Practicum in Adult English Language Teaching I and II; Language Program Design; Language Testing & Evaluation	Academic Writing; Intro. to Language & Linguistics; Structure of English; Intercultural Communication; Intro. to TESOL; Materials Evaluation & Preparation; Communicating Values Through TESOL; Second Language Acquisition; Practicum in TESOL; Advanced Methods & Techniques in TESOL; Language Testing & Assessment; Research Seminar	English Phonology; English Syntax; Language Acquisition; History of the English Language; Language & Culture; ESL Curriculum; ESL Materials & Methods I: Listening & Speaking; ESL Materials & Methods II: Reading & Writing; Evaluation in ESL; Practicum in TESL
Summer Courses	Limited offerings		Varies
OTHER		Also has M.A. in Applied Linguistics	

INSTITUTION	Cedarville College Merlin Ager, Chair, Education Box 601 Cedarville, OH 45314 Tel: (513) 766-7780 E-mail: agerm@cedarville.edu	Columbia International University Nancy S. Cheek, Dir., TEFL Program 7435 Monticello Rd. Columbia, SC 29230 Tel: (803) 754-4100, x3458 E-mail: cheekciu@aol.com	Dallas Theological Seminary Dianne Whittle, World Missions and Intercultural Studies 3909 Swiss Ave. Dallas, TX 75204 Tel: (214) 841-3684 E-mail: dianne_whittle@dts.edu
PROGRAMS **Master's**		M.A. with concentration in TEFL/ Intercultural Studies (68 sem. hrs)	
Certificate		Certificate, TEFL (12 sem. hrs)	Certificate, TESL (grad., 16 sem. hrs)
Elem./Secondary Teacher Certification	Ohio ESL Teacher Endorsement: English Ed., Elementary Ed., Spanish Ed. (30 quarter hrs)		
Undergrad. Major			
Undergrad. Minor		Minor, TEFL (15 sem. hrs)	
Course Title(s)	Intercultural Communications; History of English Language; Advanced English Grammar; Linguistics for Language Learning; Sociolinguistics; Teaching Foreign Languages Practicum	Linguistics I & II; Intro. to TEFL; Techniques of TEFL: Listening, Speaking & Reading; Techniques of TEFL: English Structure & Writing; Language Program Design; Intercultural Studies; TEFL Practicum	English Language Systems; Cross-Cultural Communication; Language Acquisition; Intro. to TESL; Teaching Listening & Speaking; Teaching Reading & Writing; Internship
Summer Courses	None	None	None
OTHER			

INSTITUTION	Eastern Mennonite University Ervie L. Glick, TESL Department 1200 Park Road Harrisonburg, VA 22801 Tel: (540) 432-4161 E-mail: glicke@emu.edu	Eastern Pentecostal Bible College Paul Kohls, Missiological Studies 780 Argyle Street Peterborough, ON K9H 5T2, Canada Tel: (705) 748-9111 E-mail: plkohls@epbc.edu	Fresno Pacific College David Freeman, Chair, Graduate Division 1717 S. Chestnut Fresno, CA 93727 Tel: (209) 453-2201 E-mail: yfreeman@fresno.edu
PROGRAMS			
Master's			M.A., TESOL (37 sem. units)
Certificate			
Elem/Secondary Teacher Certification			
Undergrad. Major			
Undergrad. Minor	Minor, TESL (18 sem. hrs)		
Course Title(s)	The English Language; Grammars of English; Psycholinguistics; Methods of TESL; TESL Practicum	Teaching English as a Second Language	Reading Process & Practice; Language Acquisition and Cross-Cultural Communication; Current Theories, Methods & Materials for Teaching a Second Language; Writing Process & Practice; Reading/Writing in the Content Areas; Practicum in TESOL; Current Theories, Methods & Materials for Bilingual Education; Cultural Diversity & Education; Intro. to Linguistics; Research in Language, Literacy & Culture; Values in School and Society
Summer Courses	Independent study	None	5 courses
OTHER		Required for Missions majors	

INSTITUTION	Goshen College Carl Barnett, English 1700 S. Main St. Goshen, IN 46526 Tel: (219) 535-7472 E-mail: carleb@goshen.edu	Grand Canyon University Bethyl Pearson, College of Education 3300 W. Camelback Glendale, AZ 85308 Tel: (602) 589-2747 E-mail: bpearso@grcanuniv.k12.az.us	Johnson Bible College Chris Templar, Teacher Education 7900 Johnson Drive Knoxville, TN 37998 Tel: (423) 579-2261 E-mail: ctemplar@jbc.edu
PROGRAMS **Master's**		M. Ed. with major in TESL (36 sem. hrs)	
Certificate	Certificate, TESOL (undergrad., 30 credits)		Certificate (undergrad.)
Elem/Secondary Teacher Certification	Indiana Teaching Endorsement (24 credits)		Tennessee Teacher Endorsement
Undergrad. Major			
Undergrad. Minor	Minor, TESOL (20 credits)		Specialty
Course Title(s)	Intro. to Linguistics; English Language Problems; TESOL Methods; TESOL Field Experience	Inter-cultural Communication; English Linguistics; English Language Teaching: Foundations & Methods; Advanced Grammar for English Language Teaching; Advanced Language Teaching: Methodologies & Assessments; Language Teaching: Curriculum & Materials Adaptation; Internship in ESL or TESL	Intro. to Linguistics; Structure of the English Language; Methods & Materials; Observation & Evaluation
Summer Courses	Limited offerings	1 course	1 course
OTHER			2 courses through distance learning

INSTITUTION	Lincoln Christian College and Seminary Miriam Windham, Christian Ministries 100 Campus View Dr. Lincoln, IL 62656 Tel: (217) 732-3168, x2292 E-mail: mwindham@prairienet.org	Moody Bible Institute Ray Badgero, Chair, World Missions and Evangelism 820 N. LaSalle Blvd. Chicago, IL 60610-3280 Tel: (312) 329-4420 E-mail: missions@moody.edu	Northwest Christian College Charles Sturms, Cross-Cultural Studies 828 E. 11th Eugene, OR 97401 Tel: (503) 343-1641
PROGRAMS **Master's**			
Certificate	Certificate (grad. & undergrad., 18 hrs)		Certificate (undergrad., 27 quarter hrs)
Elem./Secondary Teacher Certification	Illinois Teacher Endorsement		
Undergrad. Major			
Undergrad. Minor	Bi-Vocational Missions		
Course Title(s)	Intro. to Linguistics; Cross-Cultural Aspects in TESOL; TESOL: Theoretical Foundations; TESOL: Methods & Materials; Assessment & Testing in ESL; TESOL Practicum	Intro. to TESL; Methods for TESL Instruction; Intro. to Language	Intro. to Linguistics; English Grammar; TESOL Theory & Methods; TESOL Practice & Application; TESOL Practicum; Dynamics of Cross-Cultural Ministry; Intercultural Communication
Summer Courses	1 course	None	None
OTHER	Courses offered on a two-year cycle		

INSTITUTION	Northwestern College Susan Johnson, Chair, Dept. of Education 3003 Snelling Ave. North St. Paul, MN 55113-1598 Tel: (612) 631-5333 E-mail: snjohnson@nwc.edu	Nyack College Eleanor J. Pease, Director, ESL 1 South Blvd. Nyack, NY 10960 Tel: (914) 358-1710, x531	Ontario Bible College Daniel Scott, Intercultural Studies 25 Ballyconnor Court Willowdale, ON M2M 4B3, Canada Tel: (416) 226-6380 E-mail: dscott@times.net
PROGRAMS			
Master's			
Certificate		Certificate (undergrad., pending NY State approval)	Certificate (undergrad., 32 hrs)
Elem/Secondary Teacher Certification	Minnesota K-12 Teacher Licensure (with ESL Education major)		
Undergrad. Major	ESL Education; ESL (Non-Licensure)	B.S., TESOL, Education Concentration or Cross-Cultural Studies Concentration	
Undergrad. Minor	ESL (Non-Licensure)	B.S., Elementary Ed., TESOL Concentration	
Course Title(s)	Intro. to Linguistics; Advanced Grammar: Syntax; Intro. to Second Language Acquisition; Language Patterns; Second-Language Literacy Skills; Language, School, & Society; Curriculum & Instruction in ESL Education; Methods of Teaching ESL K-6; Methods of Teaching ESL 7-12; Cultural Anthropology; Intercultural Communication; Adolescent/ Adult ESL Teaching Methods; ESL Internship	General Methods in TESOL; Methods in TESOL - Language Arts; Methods in Teaching Reading; TESOL Materials; Second Language Acquisition; Nature of Language; English Grammar & Phonology; History of English Language; Multicultural Education	Fundamentals of TESL; Theoretical Foundations for TESL; Teaching ESL Communicatively; TESL Practicum
Summer Courses	Varies	None	1 course
OTHER			

INSTITUTION	Oral Roberts University Hallett Hullinger, Coordinator, Graduate TESL Program, Grad. School of Educ. 7777 South Lewis Avenue Tulsa, OK 74171-0001; Tel: (918) 497-7073 E-mail: gradedu@oru.edu	Point Loma Nazarene College Enedina Martinez, Teacher Education 3900 Lomaland Dr. San Diego, CA 92106-2899 Tel: (619) 849-2491 E-mail: enedinamartinez@oa.ptloma.edu	Seattle Pacific University Kathryn Bartholomew, Program Director 3307 Third Ave. West Seattle, WA 98119 Tel: (206) 281-2670
PROGRAMS			
Master's	M.A., Education/TESL (36 sem. hrs)	Multicultural Educ./Cross-Cultural and Academic Development (CLAD) Cert.	M.A., TESOL (54 credits)
Certificate		CLAD Certificate	
Elem/Secondary Teacher Certification		CLAD Emphasis Credential (K-12) for California pre-service teachers	
Undergrad. Major			
Undergrad. Minor	Part of International/Community Development		
Course Title(s)	Cross-Cultural Communication; Intro. to Ling.; Applied Phonetics; TESL Methods & Materials; TESL Curriculum & Methods; TESL Practicum; Structure of American English; TESL Assessment; Graduate Education Seminar	Schools & Communities in a Pluralistic Society; Structure, Acquisition & Role of Language; Bilingual Education Methodology & English Language Methodology; Research, Field Studies & Special Topics in Education; Multicultural Education; Language Structure & First/Second Language Acquisition	Phonology; Morphology; Transformational Syntax; Second Language Acquisition; Language Development & Literacy; Cultural Communication; Methodology of Foreign Language Teaching; Testing & Curriculum Development; Teaching ESL Grammar; Teaching ESL Reading; Teaching ESL Listening & Speaking; Teaching ESL Writing; Language Learning (practicum); Language Teaching (practicum)
Summer Courses	6 courses	None	6-9 courses
OTHER			2 prerequisites: linguistic theory, foreign language

INSTITUTION	Toccoa Falls College	Wheaton College Graduate School
	Timothy C. Tennent, Cross-Cultural Studies P.O. Box 800723 Toccoa Falls, GA 30598 Tel: (706) 886-6831 E-mail: ttennent@toccoafalls.edu	Alan Seaman, TESL Coordinator, Missions & Intercultural Studies Wheaton, IL 60187 Tel: (630) 752-7044 E-mail: aseaman@wheaton.edu
PROGRAMS		
Master's		M.A., Missions/Intercultural Studies with Certificate in TESL
Certificate		Certificate, TESL (grad., 24 sem. hrs)
Elem./Secondary Teacher Certification		
Undergrad. Major	Cross-Cultural Studies with concentration in TESOL	
Undergrad. Minor	Minor, TESOL (15 sem. hrs)	
Course Title(s)	Intro. to TESOL; TESOL Methods & Materials; TESOL Practicum; Language Acquisition & Development; Cross-Cultural Communication	Intro. to Linguistics; Theoretical Foundations of TESL/TEFL Methodology; Descriptive English Grammar for ESL/EFL Teachers; Curriculum & Materials Development for TESL/TEFL; Teaching Reading & Composition to ESL/EFL Learners; English Phonology for ESL/EFL Teachers; Principles of ESL/EFL Testing; Foundations of Intercultural Communication; Cross-Cultural Teaching & Learning; ESL/EFL Practicum; Teaching ESL to Children, K-12; TESL Internship
Summer Courses	1 course	5-6 courses
OTHER	Major integrates Bible, missions, anthropology, TESOL	Institute for Cross-Cultural Training offers summer courses

3. Overseas Teaching Opportunities

Students and others looking for EFL-teaching positions often ask questions such as these: Can I find a job as a Christian tentmaker? Where do I begin looking? Are there professional organizations and secular resources to help me? What about Christian organizations with overseas personnel? Is there a place for short-term teachers or summer volunteers? This chapter addresses these questions, includes three charts that show the findings of our 1996 survey of Christian organizations with openings for EFL teachers, and ends with a discussion of the survey results.

What types of positions are available for Christian tentmakers?

English teaching opportunities for Christian tentmakers are legion. Many universities are eager to hire native speakers who have a master's degree and teaching experience. Language institutes, government agencies, and international corporations often need English teachers to help their employees gain the language proficiency required for communication with others whose only common language is English. Diplomats, business executives, and students want native speakers with whom they can develop their conversational skills.

Employment Resources. Among the secular resources that address a range of employment concerns are the first four publications listed below from TESOL (address at the end of Chapter 4) and other miscellaneous works:

The ESL/EFL Job Search Handbook presents a step-by-step approach to help teachers analyze their skills and interests, plan their job search, write resumes and cover letters, handle interviews, negotiate job offers, and manage their first year of teaching.

Making a Career Choice is a packet of materials focusing on employment issues such as qualifications and credentials for teaching ESL/EFL, information on specific countries, and job placement information. The packet also includes selected articles from the *TESOL Placement Bulletin*.

TESOL Placement Bulletin. Published bimonthly by TESOL's Placement Services, this bulletin lists hundreds of available teaching positions. It also offers other useful information and advice for job seekers. For an annual fee, TESOL members can receive this bulletin and have a resume put on file.

Teaching EFL Outside the United States. Updated frequently, this handbook presents teaching opportunities and employment conditions in Africa, Asia, Europe, Latin America, and the Middle East.

The ELT Guide by Paul Lakin, ed. Published annually, this guide provides information on a wide range of teaching opportunities in more than 100 countries. For 70 countries, it provides a list of schools that hire EFL teachers and discusses practical issues of concern to those who are looking for secular employment (e.g., overview of opportunities, professional qualifications required, visas and work permits, cost of living, salaries and taxes, accommodations, health insurance, required inoculations, English language newspapers, important cultural differences and other useful information). Available from *EFL Gazette*, 10 Wrights Lane, London W8 6TA, United Kingdom, and from Delta Systems (address at the end of Chapter 4).

Teaching English Abroad by Susan Griffith. Spanning more than 200 of this book's 320 pages, the country-by-country guide provides an extensive list of teaching opportunities in Western Europe, Eastern Europe, the Middle East, Africa, Asia, and Latin America. It also includes guidance for finding a teaching position and dealing with a range of employment issues. Distributed by Peterson's Guides, Inc., 202 Carnegie Center, Princeton, NJ 08543; published by Vacation Work, 9 Park End Street, Oxford, United Kingdom.

You can also find a number of openings through electronic mail lists and the World Wide Web. On each of these forums, there are usually daily additions of new position announcements, inquiries about specific countries, and discussions about working conditions and requirements for employment. (See Chapter 5.)

What opportunities are available with mission agencies and Christian organizations?

A large number of mission agencies and Christian organizations are looking for people to teach EFL, either full time or part time. To learn more about available opportunities, we sent a questionnaire to over 250 mission organizations and other Christian groups in the United States and Canada. Of those who returned the questionnaire, more than 65 indicated that they have EFL-teaching openings or anticipate openings during the next two years. These affirmative responses were of two types: those who wanted to be listed in this handbook and those who asked not to be listed. This latter group includes agencies that send out teachers through other Christian organizations, those that have only a minimal involvement in EFL teaching, and those that do not wish to list their opportunities because their personnel work in countries officially closed to the gospel.

Need for teachers. Based on the survey forms returned, the demand for Christian EFL teachers far exceeds the supply. Of those respondents with an EFL ministry option, almost 20% anticipate needing 100 or more teachers in the next two years. The three organizations with the greatest number of teaching opportunities are the Southern Baptist Foreign Mission Board (SBFMB), English Language Institute/China (ELIC), and Educational Services International (ESI). The table below lists the approximate number of their personnel who teach English at this time and the number they would like to have in the next two years. Many of these teaching positions are short-term or summer opportunities.

	SBFMB	ELIC	ESI
EFL teachers today	350-500	375	200
EFL teachers needed	500-700	500	200

**Organizations with Greatest
Need for EFL Teachers**

1996 survey. The data in this chapter is based on the returned questionnaires from the Christian organizations that asked to be included in our survey.[1] As you look over the information in the three charts, keep in mind that career opportunities (Chart I) usually consist of a series of four-year terms, short-term opportunities (Chart II) refer to approximately three months to two years, and summer opportunities (Chart III) range from only a few days to three months. On each of the charts, we list (1) the organization, (2) the countries where they have personnel teaching English, (3) the types of teaching assignments and other responsibilities, (4) recommended professional preparation, and (5) other relevant information.[2] To contact these organizations, you can use the addresses, telephone numbers, and fax numbers listed at the end of the chapter.

---

[1]To include as many organizations as possible, we sent a second survey form to those that did not respond within three months of the first questionnaire. Those omitted from this volume, but wishing to be included in the next edition, should contact the authors. There is no charge for the listing.

[2]Although we do not list the full range of requirements for each organization, they include spiritual maturity, the ability to minister across cultures, missiological training, etc.

Chart I: Career Opportunities for EFL Teachers

ORGANIZATION	COUNTRIES	TEACHING	PREPARATION		OTHER
			Required	Recomm.	
AFRICA INLAND MISSION	Comoro Islands, Kenya, Tanzania, Zaire	A, E, L	3	1, 2, 4, 5, 6	
ARAB WORLD MINISTRIES	North Africa, Middle East	A, E, J, K	1, 2	1, 2, 3, 4, 5, 6	
CAMA SERVICES AND INTERNATIONAL FELLOWSHIP OF ALLIANCE PROFESSIONALS	China, Vietnam	A, C, M, O	1, 3	1, 2, 4, 5, 6	overseas employed professionals
CAMPUS CRUSADE FOR CHRIST	mostly creative-access countries	E, J, K, schools for MKs	3	2, 5, 6	
CBINTERNATIONAL	Poland, Ukraine	B, H, O	1, 2	1, 2, 3, 5, 6	
CHINA EDUCATIONAL EXCHANGE	China	A, L, M, N, O	2, 3	2, 5	
THE CHRISTIAN AND MISSIONARY ALLIANCE		A, B, F, G, J	2, 3		language learning required
EASTERN MENNONITE MISSIONS	Asia, Eastern Europe	A, B, D	3	1, 2, 5, 6	
EDUCATIONAL RESOURCES AND REFERRALS—CHINA	China	A, C, E	3	1, 2, 4, 5, 6	language learning required
ENGLISH LANGUAGE INSTITUTE/CHINA	China, Mongolia, Vietnam	A, C, L, M, O	3, 5	1, 2, 4, 6	language study options
EVANGELICAL FREE CHURCH MISSION	Japan, Poland, Russia	A, D, H, I	1, 3		

KEY FOR TYPES OF TEACHING ASSIGNMENTS AND OTHER RESPONSIBILITIES		KEY FOR TESL/TEFL PREPARATION
A college/university B language institute C business/technology institute D Bible college/seminary E primary/secondary school F English camp for adults G English camp for children H church program/adults	I church program/children J tutoring adults K tutoring children L teacher training M curriculum development N materials development O program administration	1 degree or certificate in TESL/TEFL 2 some course work in TESL/TEFL 3 bachelor's in any field 4 master's in any field 5 teaching exper. in ESL/EFL 6 teaching exper. in any area

ORGANIZATION	COUNTRIES	TEACHING	PREPARATION Required	PREPARATION Recomm.	OTHER
FOOD FOR THE HUNGRY	China, Japan, Laos, Vietnam	E, H, I, M, N, O		5, 6	
FRONTIERS	restricted-access countries	A, B, C, E, G, J, O		1, 5	
GREATER EUROPE MISSION	Czech Republic, Latvia, Portugal, Romania	E, F, H, J	2	1, 3, 4, 5, 6	
HARVESTING IN SPANISH	El Salvador	E, J, K, M	3	1, 2, 4, 5, 6	
INTERNATIONAL MESSENGERS	Czech Republic, Hungary, Latvia, Poland, Romania, Slovakia, Ukraine	A, B, D, F, G, J, K			
INTERNATIONAL MISSIONS, INC.		A, D, E, F, G, I, J, K		6	
INTERNATIONAL TEAMS	Austria, Czech Republic, England, France, Greece, Germany, Poland, others	F, G, J, English for refugees	2	5, 6	
INTERSERVE	Afghanistan, Bangladesh, Central Asia, China, Middle East, Nepal, Pakistan	A, B, C, E, H, L, M, O, private secular businesses	2, 3	1, 5, 6	
JAPANESE EVANGELICAL MISSIONARY SOCIETY	Japan	H, I	3, 5, 6	1	
LITERACY AND EVANGELISM INTERNATIONAL	Brazil	F, H, J	2, 3, 5	1, 6	
MENNONITE BOARD OF MISSIONS	China	A, C	2, 3	1, 4, 5, 6	
MIDDLE EAST CHRISTIAN OUTREACH		A, B, E, J, K	2, 3, 6	1, 4	
MISSION TO THE WORLD	Germany, Japan, Poland, Portugal, Taiwan, Ukraine	A, B, E, J, L		2	
MISSION TO UNREACHED PEOPLES	Asia (Japan, Taiwan, others), Poland	A, E, F, G, H, I, J, K, L, M, N, O	3	1, 2, 4, 6	

Organization	Countries	Teaching	Preparation Required	Preparation Recomm.	Other
NETWORK OF INTERNATIONAL CHRISTIAN SCHOOLS	Korea, Thailand	B, E, H, I, L, M, O	3	1, 2, 4, 5, 6	1-3 year contracts
NEXUS/WORLD TEAM	Indonesia, Cambodia	A, B, L	1	2, 3, 4, 5, 6	
OMF INTERNATIONAL	Cambodia, China, Japan, Korea, Thailand, Vietnam	A, C, H, church program for students	1, 3, 5	1	
OMS INTERNATIONAL	Ecuador, Hong Kong, Hungary, Korea, Mexico	A, D, G, H, L, M, N, O	1, 2, 3	4, 5, 6	
OPERATION MOBILIZATION	Central Asia, Central Europe, Middle East, North Africa	A, B, E	1	5	
PIONEERS	China, Indonesia, Japan, Thailand, others	A, B, J		1, 2, 3, 4, 5, 6	
RUSSIAN-AMERICAN CHRISTIAN UNIVERSITY	Russia	A, B, L, M, N	1, 4, 5		
SEND INTERNATIONAL	East Asia, Hong Kong, Japan	G, I, J, K, L, N, O	1, 3	5, 6	
SIM INTERNATIONAL	Benin, Ecuador, Eritrea, Ethiopia, Mongolia, Pakistan, Paraguay	A, B, D, E, I, J, K	1, 3, 6	1, 2, 5, 6	language learning required
SOUTHERN BAPTIST FOREIGN MISSION BOARD	more than 175 countries	A, B, C, D, H, I, J, K, L, M, N, O	1, 2, 3		

KEY FOR TYPES OF TEACHING ASSIGNMENTS AND OTHER RESPONSIBILITIES		KEY FOR TESL/TEFL PREPARATION
A college/university B language institute C business/technology institute D Bible college/seminary E primary/secondary school F English camp for adults G English camp for children H church program/adults	I church program/children J tutoring adults K tutoring children L teacher training M curriculum development N materials development O program administration	1 degree or certificate in TESL/TEFL 2 some course work in TESL/TEFL 3 bachelor's in any field 4 master's in any field 5 teaching exper. in ESL/EFL 6 teaching exper. in any area

Organization	Countries	Teaching	Preparation		Other
			Required	*Recomm.*	
TEAM	Austria, China, Czech Republic, Japan, Hong Kong/Macau, Poland, Portugal, Russia, Taiwan, Venezuela, others	A, B, C, E, F, G, H, J, K, L, M, N, O	varies	varies	
UFM INTERNATIONAL	Brazil, Dominican Republic, Mexico	A, D, E, G	2, 3, 5	1	
WEC INTERNATIONAL		A, B, C, D, J, K, L, M, N, O	2, 5, 6	1, 2, 3, 4, 5	

Chart II: Short-Term Opportunities for EFL Teachers

ORGANIZATION	COUNTRIES	TEACHING	PREPARATION		OTHER
			Required	Recomm.	
AFRICA INLAND MISSION	Comoro Islands, Kenya, Tanzania, Zaire	E		1, 2, 3, 4, 5, 6	
BAPTIST GENERAL CONFERENCE WORLD MISSIONS	Japan, Thailand, Vietnam	A, C, F, H, I		4	
CAMA SERVICES AND INTERNATIONAL FELLOWSHIP OF ALLIANCE PROFESSIONALS	Cambodia, China, Indonesia, Vietnam	A, C, D, E	3	1, 2, 4, 5, 6	overseas employed professionals
CAMPUS CRUSADE FOR CHRIST	mostly creative access countries	E, J, K, schools for MKs	3		
CBINTERNATIONAL	Indonesia, Japan, Macau, Madagascar, Poland, Portugal, Russia, Spain, Taiwan, Ukraine, others	A, B, F, H, M, O	1, 2	1, 2, 3, 5, 6	
CHINA EDUCATIONAL EXCHANGE	China	A	3	2, 5	
CHRISTIAN REFORMED WORLD MISSION	China, Hungary, Romania, Ukraine				
EDUCATIONAL RESOURCES AND REFERRALS—CHINA	China	A, C, E	3	1, 2, 4, 5, 6	
EDUCATIONAL SERVICES INTERNATIONAL	Central Asia, China, Czech Republic, Hungary, Romania, Russia, Siberia, Ukraine	A, B, E, O	3	6	native English speaker

KEY FOR TYPES OF TEACHING ASSIGNMENTS AND OTHER RESPONSIBILITIES		KEY FOR TESL/TEFL PREPARATION
A college/university	I church program/children	1 degree or certificate in TESL/TEFL
B language institute	J tutoring adults	2 some course work in TESL/TEFL
C business/technology institute	K tutoring children	3 bachelor's in any field
D Bible college/seminary	L teacher training	4 master's in any field
E primary/secondary school	M curriculum development	5 teaching exper. in ESL/EFL
F English camp for adults	N materials development	6 teaching exper. in any area
G English camp for children	O program administration	
H church program/adults		

Organization	Countries	Teaching	Preparation Required	Preparation Recomm.	Other
ENGLISH LANGUAGE INSTITUTE/CHINA	China, Mongolia, Vietnam	A, C, E, O	3	1, 2, 4, 5, 6	
EVANGELICAL FREE CHURCH MISSION	Japan, Poland, Russia	D, H, I	3	2, 5, 6	
FOOD FOR THE HUNGRY	China, Japan, Laos, Vietnam	E, H, I, M, N, O		5, 6	
FREE METHODIST WORLD MISSIONS	Dominican Republic, Hungary, Japan, Taiwan	A, B	3	5, 6	
FRONTIERS	restricted-access countries	A, B, C, E, F, G, J, O		1, 5	
GRACE BRETHREN INTERNATIONAL MISSIONS	Brazil, Cambodia, Central African Republic, France, Japan, Thailand	B, J, English clubs		5, 6	
GREATER EUROPE MISSION	Czech Republic, Latvia, Romania	E, F, H, J, K		1, 2, 3, 4, 5, 6	
HARVESTING IN SPANISH	El Salvador	E, J, K, M	3	1, 2, 4, 5, 6	
INTERNATIONAL MESSENGERS	Czech Republic, Hungary, Latvia, Poland, Romania, Slovakia, Ukraine	F, G, J, K			
INTERNATIONAL MISSIONS, INC.		A, D, E, F, G, H, I, J, K	3	4, 6	
INTERNATIONAL TEAMS	Austria, Czech Republic, England, France, Greece, Germany, Poland, others	F, G, J, English for refugees	2, 3, 6	5, 6	
INTERSERVE	Central Asia, China, Middle East, Pakistan	B, C, H, J, K	varies	1, 2, 3, 5	
JAPANESE EVANGELICAL MISSIONARY SOCIETY	Japan	H, I, J, K	6	3, 5	
LITERACY AND EVANGELISM INTERNATIONAL	Brazil, Ecuador, Indonesia, Pakistan, Thailand	B, F, J, L	5	2, 6	

Organization	Countries	Teaching	Preparation Required	Preparation Recomm.	Other
Lutheran Bible Translators	Namibia	E, H, J, L, N	2, 3, 6	4, 5	
Mennonite Board of Missions	China	A, C	2, 3	1, 4, 5, 6	
Mennonite Brethren/Missions Services	Japan, Thailand	H, I		3, 5	
Mennonite Central Committee	Angola, China, Egypt, Vietnam	A, B, D, E, J, K, L, M, N	1, 3	1, 2, 5, 6	
Middle East Christian Outreach		B, D, J, K	3, 6		
Mission to the World	Czech Republic, Germany, Japan, Poland, Portugal, Taiwan, Ukraine	A, B, E, J, K, L		2	
Mission to Unreached Peoples	Asia (Japan, Taiwan, others), Poland	F, G, H, I, J, K		1, 2, 3, 4, 5, 6	
Network of International Christian Schools	Korea, Thailand	B, E	3	1, 2, 4, 5, 6	
Nexus/World Team	Cambodia, Indonesia	A, B	1, 5	2, 3, 4, 6	
Okinawa Christian School Mission	Japan	B, E, F, G, H, I, L, M, N, O	3	1, 2, 4, 6	
OMF International	China, Japan, Korea, Thailand	A, C, H	1, 3, 5		

KEY FOR TYPES OF TEACHING ASSIGNMENTS AND OTHER RESPONSIBILITIES		KEY FOR TESL/TEFL PREPARATION
A college/university **B** language institute **C** business/technology institute **D** Bible college/seminary **E** primary/secondary school **F** English camp for adults **G** English camp for children **H** church program/adults	**I** church program/children **J** tutoring adults **K** tutoring children **L** teacher training **M** curriculum development **N** materials development **O** program administration	**1** degree or certificate in TESL/TEFL **2** some course work in TESL/TEFL **3** bachelor's in any field **4** master's in any field **5** teaching exper. in ESL/EFL **6** teaching exper. in any area

Organization	Countries	Teaching	Preparation		Other
			Required	Recomm.	
OMS International	Ecuador, Hong Kong, Hungary, Korea, Mexico, Taiwan	A, G, H, L, O	3	1, 2, 4, 5, 6	
Operation Mobilization	Central Asia, Central Europe, Middle East, North Africa	A, B, E	2	5	
Pioneers	varies	A, B, J		2, 3, 6	
Russian-American Christian University	Russia	A, B, L	1, 5	4	
SEND International	Bulgaria, East Asia, Hong Kong, Japan, Philippines, Ukraine	D, F, H, I, J, K, N, O		3, 5, 6	
SIM International	Benin, Ecuador, Eritrea, Ethiopia, Korea, Pakistan, Paraguay	A, D, E, J, K	1, 3, 6	1, 2, 5, 6	
Southern Baptist Foreign Mission Board	more than 175 countries	A, B, C, D, E, F, G	3	1, 2	
TEAM	Austria, Czech Republic, Japan, Hong Kong/Macau, Portugal, Taiwan, Venezuela, others	A, B, C, E, F, G, H, J, K	varies	varies	
UFM International	Brazil, Dominican Republic, Mexico	A, D, E, G	2, 3, 5	1	

Chart III: Summer Opportunities for EFL Teachers

Organization	Countries	Teaching	Preparation Required	Preparation Recomm.	Other
Baptist General Conference World Missions	Japan, Thailand	A, F, H		4	
CAMA Services and International Fellowship of Alliance Professionals		A, D, E	3	2, 6	overseas employed professionals
CBInternational	varies	A		1, 2, 3, 5, 6	
Eastern Mennonite Missions	Eastern Europe	A, B	3		
Educational Resources and Referrals—China	China	A, E, J			20+ years old
Educational Services International	China, Russia	A, G			2 years college, native English speaker
English Language Institute/China	China, Mongolia, Vietnam	A, C, L, O		1, 2, 3, 4, 5, 6	
Evangelical Free Church Mission	Belgium, Brazil, Czech Republic, Hong Kong, Slovakia, Venezuela	F, G			
Grace Brethren International Missions	Brazil, Cambodia, Central African Republic, France, Japan, Thailand	J			

KEY FOR TYPES OF TEACHING ASSIGNMENTS AND OTHER RESPONSIBILITIES		KEY FOR TESL/TEFL PREPARATION
A college/university	I church program/children	1 degree or certificate in TESL/TEFL
B language institute	J tutoring adults	2 some course work in TESL/TEFL
C business/technology institute	K tutoring children	3 bachelor's in any field
D Bible college/seminary	L teacher training	4 master's in any field
E primary/secondary school	M curriculum development	5 teaching exper. in ESL/EFL
F English camp for adults	N materials development	6 teaching exper. in any area
G English camp for children	O program administration	
H church program/adults		

ORGANIZATION	COUNTRIES	TEACHING	PREPARATION		OTHER
			Required	Recomm.	
GREATER EUROPE MISSION	Latvia, Ukraine	F, H, J			in-house training
HARVESTING IN SPANISH	El Salvador	J, K, M, N	2	1, 3, 4, 5, 6	
INTERNATIONAL MESSENGERS	Czech Republic, Hungary, Latvia, Poland, Romania, Slovakia, Ukraine	F, G			
INTERNATIONAL MISSIONS, INC.		A, D, F, G, H, I, J, K	3	4	
INTERNATIONAL TEAMS	Austria, Czech Republic, England, France, Greece, Germany, Poland, others	F, G, J, English for refugees		6	
INTERSERVE	Central Asia, China, Pakistan	B, C, H, J, K	varies	1, 2, 3, 5	18+ years old
JAPANESE EVANGELICAL MISSIONARY SOCIETY	Brazil, Japan	G, H, I	6	5	
LITERACY AND EVANGELISM INTERNATIONAL	Belize, Brazil, Kenya, Mexico, Pakistan, Zaire	G, J	5	6	curriculum provided
OMF INTERNATIONAL	China, Japan, Thailand				training & curriculum provided
OMS INTERNATIONAL	Ecuador, Hong Kong, Hungary, Korea, Mexico, Taiwan, Spain	G, H		2, 3, 5, 6	
OPERATION MOBILIZATION	Central Asia	B	2	5	
PIONEERS	varies	B, J		2, 6	
RUSSIAN-AMERICAN CHRISTIAN UNIVERSITY	Russia	A, B	1, 5	4	
SEND INTERNATIONAL	Czech Republic, Macedonia, Philippines, Poland	F, G, H, J, M, N			
SIM INTERNATIONAL	Korea	B, D		5, 6	

ORGANIZATION	COUNTRIES	TEACHING	PREPARATION		OTHER
			Required	Recomm.	
SOUTHERN BAPTIST FOREIGN MISSION BOARD	more than 175 countries	A, B, C, F		5, 6	
TEAM	Czech Republic, Japan, Russia, Taiwan, Venezuela	A, B, F, G, H, I, J, K	varies	varies	
UFM INTERNATIONAL	Brazil, Dominican Republic, France, Mexico	A, D, E, G	2	1	

KEY FOR TYPES OF TEACHING ASSIGNMENTS AND OTHER RESPONSIBILITIES		KEY FOR TESL/TEFL PREPARATION
A college/university **B** language institute **C** business/technology institute **D** Bible college/seminary **E** primary/secondary school **F** English camp for adults **G** English camp for children **H** church program/adults	**I** church program/children **J** tutoring adults **K** tutoring children **L** teacher training **M** curriculum development **N** materials development **O** program administration	**1** degree or certificate in TESL/TEFL **2** some course work in TESL/TEFL **3** bachelor's in any field **4** master's in any field **5** teaching exper. in ESL/EFL **6** teaching exper. in any area

Discussion of survey results. A closer look at charts I-III reveals some interesting, and not entirely obvious, facts that may affect your choice of teaching opportunities under the auspices of Christian organizations. Your choice, in turn, may affect the preparation you pursue.

Countries in which English is in greatest demand. Although there are opportunities to teach EFL in many different countries, our survey shows that openings predominate in Asia (particularly China) and in Eastern Europe and the former Soviet Union. You should keep in mind, however, that these charts do not list every location where a Christian organization may want to place teachers. Therefore, if you are interested in another part of the world, you may want to explore your preferences with these same agencies. Alternatively, you may find other Christian groups with opportunities for EFL teaching or tutoring in the location you have in mind.[1] Or, you may want to consult the secular employment sources cited earlier in this chapter.

Teaching situations in which opportunities are most plentiful. While EFL-teaching needs are apparent at all levels of the educational system and with adults as well as children, our survey shows that you may find the job search easier if you want to teach adults, especially at the college and university level. This is true for short-term and summer assignments as well as for career openings, as indicated in the table below. Language institutes are also likely places for employment, as are primary and secondary schools for career and short-term teachers. In addition, opportunities to tutor adults are plentiful, often as a part-time ministry for those working in other capacities.

	Career	Short-Term	Summer
college/university	75%	48%	44%
language institute	47%	38%	30%
primary/secondary school	39%	43%	11%
tutoring adults	42%	38%	41%

Teaching Situations in Highest Demand

The percentages listed above are based on the number of agencies and organizations that checked each type of teaching opportunity; they do not reflect the total number of positions available in each situation.

Specialized teaching responsibilities. On the three major charts, four types of responsibilities in the "Teaching" category require special training and skills (letters L, M, N, O): teacher training, curriculum development, materials development, and program administration. The need for teachers with these strengths, however, is not evenly distributed across the three periods of service—career, short-term, and summer. As the next table shows, only a few (11%) of the summer positions require one or more of these specialized abilities, while almost one-half (47%) of the agencies and organizations reported that some of their career personnel must deal with one or more of these four responsibilities. About one-fourth (26%) have some short-term personnel handling at least one of these specialized tasks. That is, the longer the term of service, the greater the range of leadership responsibilities and the greater the need for strong preparation through EFL course work and teaching experience.

		Career	Short-Term	Summer
L	teacher training			
M	curriculum development	47%	26%	11%
N	materials development			
O	program administration			

Specialized Teaching Responsibilities

---

[1]You can find additional mission agencies listed in *The Great Commission Handbook, The Short-Term Mission Handbook,* and *MISSION TODAY,* available from Berry Publishing Services, Inc., 701 Main Street, Evanston, IL 60202, Telephone: (847) 869-1573, Fax: (847) 869-4825.

Required preparation. The following table highlights the importance that Christian organizations place on the six categories of required preparation listed in our survey. For each category, it shows the percentage of organizations that require a specific type or level of preparation for at least some of their EFL teachers. The table refines the observation above: more is expected in the way of preparation for EFL teaching as the period of service lengthens. For example, while a large number of organizations require their career and short-term EFL teachers to have a bachelor's degree (61%, career; 50%, short-term), many summer teaching opportunities are open to students and others without degrees. Nevertheless, there is still a strong expectation that all teachers have "some course work in TESL/TEFL" and "ESL/EFL teaching experience." This expectation of preparedness increases with short-term and career teachers to include a "degree or certificate in TESL/TEFL." We believe that the percentage of organizations who want their EFL teachers to have course work, teaching experience, and a degree or certificate in the field will increase each time a new survey is conducted.

	Career	Short-Term	Summer
degree or certificate in TESL/TEFL	32%	15%	8%
some course work in TESL/TEFL	41%	23%	19%
bachelor's degree in any field	61%	50%	11%
master's degree in any field	3%	0%	0%
teaching experience in ESL/EFL	21%	13%	8%
teaching experience in any area	12%	10%	4%

Required Preparation

Summary. How should you interpret these survey results? There are hundreds of opportunities for Christians to teach English overseas, with a need for EFL teachers in almost every country and at all levels of instruction. Appropriate teacher training opens the doors to the widest range of teaching positions. We believe that mission agencies and other Christian organizations, like their secular counterparts worldwide, are increasingly recognizing the importance of well-prepared EFL teachers. They are the ones who are most likely to make a significant contribution to an EFL-teaching ministry.

Addresses and telephone numbers for mission agencies and other Christian organizations

Africa Inland Mission
P.O. Box 178
Pearl River, NY 10965
(914) 735-4014

Arab World Ministries
P.O. Box 96
Upper Darby, PA 19082

Baptist General Conference World Missions
2002 S. Arlington Heights Road
Arlington Heights, IL 60005
(847) 228-0200

CAMA Services and International Fellowship of Alliance Professionals
Box 35000
Colorado Springs, CO 80935-3500
(719) 599-5999

P. O. Box 7900, Station B
Willowdale, ON M2K 2R6
Canada
(416) 492-8775

Campus Crusade for Christ International
100 Sunport Lane
Orlando, FL 32809
(407) 826-2822

CBInternational
P. O. Box 5
Wheaton, IL 60189-0005
(630) 260-3800

China Educational Exchange
1251 Virginia Avenue
Harrisonburg, VA 22801
(540) 432-6983

The Christian and Missionary Alliance
Box 35000
Colorado Springs, CO 80935-3500
(719) 599-5999

P. O. Box 7900, Station B
Willowdale, ON M2K 2R6
Canada
(416) 492-8775

Christian Reformed World Missions
2850 Kalamazoo Avenue, SE
Grand Rapids, MI 49560
(616) 224-0703

Eastern Mennonite Missions
Oak Lane and Brandt Blvd.
P. O. Box 628
Salunga, PA 17538-0628
(717) 898-2251

Educational Resources and Referrals—China
2606 Dwight Way
Berkeley, CA 94704
(510) 548-7519

Educational Services International
1641 W. Main Street, #401
Alhambra, CA 91801
(800) 895-7955

English Language Institute/China
P.O. Box 265
San Dimas, CA 91773
(800) 366-3542

Evangelical Free Church Mission
901 E. 78th Street
Minneapolis, MN 55420
(612) 854-1300

Food for the Hungry
7729 E. Greenway Road
Scottsdale, AZ 85260
(800) 2-HUNGER

Free Methodist World Missions
P. O. Box 535002
Indianapolis, IN 46253-5002
(317) 244-3660

Frontiers
325 N. Stapley Drive
Mesa, AZ 85203
(602) 834-1500

Grace Brethren International Missions
P. O. Box 588
Winona Lake, IN 46590
(219) 268-1888

Greater Europe Mission
18950 Base Camp Road
Monument, CO 80922
(719) 488-8008

Harvesting in Spanish
Amilat 723 Box 52-5364
Miami, FL 33152-5364
011-503-226-2130 (El Salvador)

International Messengers
110 Orchard Court, P. O. Box R
Clear Lake, IA 50428
(515) 357-6700

International Missions, Inc.
Box 14866
Reading, PA 19612-4866
(610) 375-0300

International Teams
P. O. Box 203
Prospect Heights, IL 60070
(847) 870-3800

InterServe
P. O. Box 418
Upper Darby, PA 19082
(610) 352-4394

10 Huntingdale Blvd.
Scarborough, ON M1W 2S5
(416) 499-7511

Japanese Evangelical Missionary Society
948 E. Second Street
Los Angeles, CA 90012
(213) 613-0022

Literacy and Evangelism International
1912 Swallow Lane
Carlsbad, CA 92009
(619) 438-4321

Lutheran Bible Translators
303 N. Lake Street
Box 2050
Aurora, IL 60507-2050
(630) 897-0660

Mennonite Board of Missions
P. O. Box 370
Elkhart, IN 46515
(219) 294-7523

Mennonite Brethren Missions Services
4867 E. Townsend
Fresno, CA 93727-5006
(209) 456-4600

Mennonite Central Committee
21 S. 12th Street
Akron, PA 17501
(717) 859-1151

Middle East Christian Outreach
P. O. Box 1008
Moorhead, MN 56561
(218) 236-5963

Mission to the World
P. O. Box 29765
Atlanta, GA 30359
(404) 320-3373

Mission to Unreached Peoples
P. O. Box 45880
Seattle, WA 98145-0880
(206) 781-3151

Network of International Christian Schools
P. O. Box 18151
Memphis, TN 38181
(901) 276-8377

Nexus/World Team
1431 Stukert Road
Warrington, PA 18976-1526
(215) 491-4900

2476 Argentia Road, #203
Mississauga, ON L5N 6M1
(905) 821-6300

Okinawa Christian School Mission
P. O. Box 90031
Gainesville, FL 32607
(800) 446-6423

OMF International
10 West Dry Creek Circle
Littleton, CO 80120-4413
(303) 730-4160

OMS International
Box A
Greenwood, IN 46142
(317) 881-6751

Operation Mobilization
P. O. Box 444
Tyrone, GA 30290-0444
(404) 631-0432

Pioneers
12343 Narcoossee Road
Orlando, FL 32827-5500
(800) 755-7284

Russian-American Christian University
U. S. Office
P. O. Box 2007
Wheaton, MD 20915-2007
(301) 681-1456

SEND International
P. O. Box 513
Farmington, MI 48332
(810) 477-4210

SIM International
P. O. Box 7900
Charlotte, NC 28241-7900
(704) 588-4300

10 Huntingdale Blvd.
Scarborough, ON M1W 2S5
Canada
(416) 497-2424

Southern Baptist Foreign Mission Board
Box 6767
Richmond, VA 23230
(804) 999-3113

TEAM
P. O. Box 969
Wheaton, IL 60189-0969
(800) 343-3144

UFM International
Box 306
Bala Cynwyd, PA 19004
(610) 667-7660

WEC International
Box 1707
Fort Washington, PA 19034
(215) 646-2322

37 Aberdeen Avenue
Hamilton, ON L8P 2N6
Canada
(416) 529-0166

4. Materials for Teachers and Learners

EFL teachers—seasoned practitioners as well as novices—often ask a host of questions about resources: What professional resources can help me become a better teacher? How do I know which books to select for my personal library? What materials should I consider for my classroom teaching? What criteria should I apply to locate the best textbooks from among the thousands of choices? Where can I find what I need?

The three major sections of this chapter offer answers to these questions. In the first, we discuss the range of teacher-preparation books designed to help you become a more competent EFL instructor. In this section, we also focus on a problem nearly all EFL teachers face—how to select the most appropriate classroom teaching/learning materials. The second section provides an annotated bibliography with a wide variety of entries for these two categories of resources (teacher-preparation books and classroom teaching/learning materials). The final section lists the addresses, phone numbers, and fax numbers for major publishers and distributors, both secular and Christian.

TEXTBOOKS

What types of teacher-preparation books are there?

If you are new to the field of EFL teaching, you may be questioning the importance of professional-preparation materials. You may not sense an immediate need to read books about language learning and teaching—especially books on theory. Most teachers, however, discover a wealth of useful knowledge and helpful guidance in the writings of the leading specialists in the field. Novice teachers can read about everyday concerns, such as how to set up a conversation class or how to foster genuine communication in the classroom. Experienced practitioners can deal with more complex issues, such as procedures for curriculum design and guidance for training new teachers. Whatever your professional concerns, you can probably find the help you need in one or more of the five categories of teacher-preparation books we list. Furthermore, as you reflect on the theoretical insights and practical ideas contained in these books, you will develop a deeper understanding of your students and their individual learning needs, and thereby become a more confident and effective EFL teacher.

Theoretical foundations. Books that provide a base of knowledge about what language is and how it is learned draw on the contributions of disciplines such as linguistics, education, and psychology to the teaching and learning of a second language. These resources offer sound theoretical underpinnings and a principled approach for the many decisions you must make as an EFL teacher.

Classroom-oriented principles and methods. Resources that serve as a bridge between second language acquisition theory and actual classroom practice contribute another important category of professional materials. Although some of these resources overlap with those in the first category (theoretical foundations), the focus here is on sound information to inform your instructional choices, from teaching approaches and methods, to language-learning strategies, to the effective use of a textbook.

Teaching resources for specific language skills. Since many EFL classes focus on only one or two skills (e.g., listening and speaking, or grammar and composition), many teacher resource books address only one specific skill or aspect of language teaching. These commonly include: teaching reading, teaching writing, teaching listening/speaking or conversation, teaching grammar, teaching English for specific purposes (e.g, Business English or Medical English), cultural aspects of learning, and testing. Some of these books provide a variety of practical activities and games that can add to your repertoire of classroom ideas.

Resource materials. Some books offer suggestions, topics, and word lists for developing supplemental activities and creating your own teacher-made materials to use in the classroom.

Reference materials. Although not necessarily ESL or EFL in orientation, certain reference works should be part of every good EFL library. Invaluable additions to your library, these books equip you with a broad understanding of the English language system, including more technical background knowledge, that you can draw upon to answer tough questions about the linguistic aspects of grammar, pronunciation, etc. Some also offer ideas for presenting the material to students in an easy-to-comprehend fashion.

How do I select classroom teaching/learning materials?

With thousands of textbooks on the market, and dozens of publishers vying for your business, the selection of appropriate classroom materials is far from a simple process. To help you make a well-informed decision, we highlight two challenges most teachers face in an overseas context and some widely held myths about EFL/ESL books. Then, we discuss four key steps to guide your evaluation of materials and selection of the most appropriate textbooks for your instructional needs.

Challenges in an EFL context. Teachers looking for materials appropriate for EFL learners are likely to encounter two challenges not shared by their ESL colleagues: the availability of textbooks and the suitability of content. First, many of the materials readily available in the United States and the United Kingdom are difficult to obtain in other parts of the world. Second, some of the available textbooks may be unsuitable in an EFL context because they focus only on the language and situations of learners living in an area where English is widely spoken (e.g., vocabulary and phrases used for shopping in an American supermarket). ESL materials such as these may be inappropriate for overseas learners who have little interest in the topics presented and no opportunity to use similar language outside the classroom.

Myths about EFL/ESL textbooks. Those new to the field of EFL teaching often subscribe to at least one of the three common myths about classroom texts. Because of their prevalence, it may be helpful if we offer a counterpoint to each one.

First, new teachers may believe the myth that "the textbook is the course." Although many excellent textbooks are available, there is no perfect textbook that can meet all the teaching-learning needs that will arise in your particular situation. The most appropriate course content is often developed by using an eclectic approach which pulls the most useful ideas and activities from a variety of resources, including one or more EFL textbooks. The textbook, then, is only one of several sources you draw on to encourage your students to learn.

The second myth is that "the textbook should be taught in its entirety with nothing added or deleted." It is seldom the wisest decision to let this myth guide your planning. The time frame of a course may not allow sufficient teaching hours to deal adequately with each lesson in the text, or the content of individual lessons may be unsuitable for your students' needs or proficiency level. Only you, as the classroom teacher, can determine which parts of a text are appropriate and useful for your EFL learners. Good advice to new teachers comes in the form of an adage: The best textbook is not the one you adopt but the one you adapt.

The final myth is that "if the title of the book contains the word 'communicative,' you can trust that it is." This word, unfortunately, has become an overused buzzword in the EFL/ESL community, and many of the textbooks claiming this orientation do not live up to their billing. Keep in mind that a truly communicative text fosters the use of English for real life tasks. Through activities such as pair work and small group work, it provides students with opportunities to use their new language in a controlled setting (e.g., classroom) before using it out of class. It also focuses on overall fluency (i.e., smoothness or "flow") as well as the accuracy of grammatical forms. Finally, a communicative textbook encourages the use of authentic everyday language instead of "textbook" language that may be stilted and unrealistic.

Textbook evaluation and selection. To make an informed decision about textbook selection, you should know some information about your students' needs, your instructional objectives, and your personal teaching preferences. We list a number of questions to guide you through this assessment process. Although you may not be able to find a satisfactory answer for each question, the answers you do find—as well as the additional information you gather in the process—will be of considerable benefit in evaluating and selecting materials appropriate for your teaching situation.

Know your students' needs. An invaluable first step in the selection of materials is to gather information about your students' language learning needs and preferences. Although you may want to collect a much wider range of information, we suggest that you begin with these four categories: (1) language background, (2) proficiency level, (3) goals, and (4) preferred approaches to learning.

Language background: previous experiences with their native language and with English

- Can they read and write in their native language?

- In what settings have they studied English (e.g., classroom, tutoring, self-study)?

Proficiency level in English

- Are they beginners, or do they already know some English?

- Are all students at the same level?

- Are they stronger in some skills (e.g., reading and writing) and weaker in others (e.g., listening and speaking)?

Learning goals

- Do they need English for reading and writing purposes, or will they use the language mostly for listening and speaking?

- If they require oral communication skills, with whom will they speak English? For example, will they use the language with other non-native English speakers, or will they use it with business executives whose native language is English?

- What tasks do they want to accomplish in English? For example, will they need the language to sell products to speakers of English, or will they need it in order to understand lectures in English?

Preferred approaches to learning

- How do they learn most easily? What is their primary orientation—visual, auditory, kinesthetic, etc.? Do they favor analytical or global learning?

- Are they accustomed to a more traditional, teacher-centered classroom in which most interaction is between teacher and student (not student to student), or are they more comfortable in a learner-centered classroom in which students interact with one another in pairs and small groups?

- Do they like language learning activities in which they have an opportunity to communicate freely even though they may make mistakes, or do they prefer the study of grammar and an emphasis on accuracy of speech and writing?

The answers to these questions will provide one type of information essential for choosing materials that are suitable for your particular students. For example, if you are a new teacher in a country where much of your students' previous instruction involved rote memorization of facts, you may not want to begin your teaching with a textbook that is strongly communicative or one that has little emphasis on grammar and accuracy. Frequently, a more communicative textbook will be better received after you have gained your students' trust, and after you have employed activities such as pair work and role play gradually over time.

Know your instructional objectives. Taking the time to clearly define your objectives—or to understand the list of objectives provided by the institution in which you teach—will greatly limit the scope of your search for the right textbook. To do this, you should ask questions such as this:

- Given my students' language background, proficiency level, learning goals, and preferred approaches to learning, what can I realistically expect them to be able to do as a result of my English instruction?

- Make a list of general objectives (e.g., speak outside of class with native English speakers) and for each, try to list two or three specific objectives (e.g., discuss everyday topics such as foods and clothing).

With a list of objectives in hand, you can narrow your textbook selection considerably. You do this by matching your objectives with the proficiency level, content focus, and activity types of a number of potential choices. You may find, for example, that your preferred text should have a heavy emphasis on grammar. Or, you may discover that it should focus entirely on oral communication skills, including pronunciation, but have little or no emphasis on grammar.

Know your personal teaching preferences. The third step in the selection process is the assessment of your own teaching style and teaching preferences. To help you to think about the teaching-learning environment that is most ideal for you, as well as your expectations of a textbook, you can begin with questions such as these:

Classroom environment: roles of teacher and students

- What teacher role(s) suit your personality and teaching style? Do you prefer the role of director (one who carefully guides students in their learning exercises and activities, usually having them interact more with you than with each other), the role of facilitator (one who organizes and monitors pair work and small group work), or some combination of these roles?

The "fit" between teaching style and textbook choice

- How dependent are you on the textbook content for planning your lessons? For example, do you prefer to stick to the textbook, using it as your basic syllabus? Or, do you like to vary your approach based on the content of the lesson?

- Are you good at adapting materials and/or creating supplemental activities?

As you examine a range of textbooks, you should look for those that accentuate your strengths while also encouraging you to develop skills in new areas. For example, if you have not taught EFL before, you may prefer to begin with a text that is more teacher-centered, allowing you to be more in control of instructional activities. Then, as you get to know your students and feel more comfortable in the classroom, you may want to adapt some of the book's activities for small group work, thus creating a more learner-centered environment.

Summary: three key questions. By carefully evaluating a number of textbooks in light of what you know about your students' needs, your instructional objectives, and yourself as a teacher, you will be better equipped to choose the best materials for your teaching-learning situation. For each of these four areas, we have given you a set of questions to guide your selection process. However, each set can be summarized by a single key question to ask about the textbook(s) you are considering.

- How appropriate is it for my students' language learning needs?

- To what extent does it focus on my instructional objectives?

- What skills do I need in order to use it most effectively?

BIBLIOGRAPHY

The following bibliography is divided into two sections: teacher-preparation books and classroom teaching/learning materials. As language teaching practices change and as new publications appear, this list will become out of date.

Teacher-preparation books

This first section, teacher-preparation books, contains many valuable resources to help you grow as an EFL professional. Each book contributes to the building of a strong foundation for your EFL classroom instruction and out-of-class tutoring. The entries are divided into five categories: theoretical foundations, classroom-oriented principles and methods, teaching resources for specific language skills, resource materials, and reference materials. This selection of books, however, is not exhaustive. Some publications have been omitted for the sake of brevity; other worthwhile entries may have been overlooked.

In order to fully utilize these resources, you should have ready access to them. For many EFL teachers, this means purchasing the books for your personal library. If you can buy only a few selections, first consider those marked with an asterisk. These publications either offer a more global discussion of issues related to language teaching/learning, or they provide highly useful suggestions and guidance for classroom teaching.

Theoretical foundations

Beebe, Leslie, Ed. 1988. *Issues in Second Language Acquisition: Multiple Perspectives.* Boston: Heinle & Heinle.

Synthesis of current second language acquisition research from five different perspectives: psycholinguistic, sociolinguistic, neurolinguistic, classroom research, and bilingual education. Specialists in each field explore the implications of these perspectives on SLA theory.

*Brown, H. Douglas. 1994. *Principles of Language Learning and Teaching.* 3rd ed. Englewood Cliffs, NJ: Prentice Hall, Inc.

Excellent analysis of the major theoretical issues. Explores topics ranging from theories of learning to differences between first and second language acquisition. Comprehensive explanation of variables that affect language learning. Extensive updated bibliography and, at the end of each chapter, ideas for classroom application.

Skehan, Peter. 1989. *Individual Differences in Second-Language Learning.* New York: Edward Arnold.

Focuses on research findings regarding key factors that impact the success or failure of language learning, including aptitude, motivation, language learning strategies, and cognitive and affective variables related to learning styles.

*Wolfson, Nessa. 1989. *Perspectives: Sociolinguistics and TESOL.* Boston: Heinle & Heinle.

Explores the growing importance of sociolinguistics within the TESOL profession. Discusses historical trends in research and provides a foundational understanding of the cross-cultural differences in speech behavior and the rules that govern verbal interaction. Equips teachers with a strong theoretical foundation for teaching conversation.

Classroom-oriented principles and methods

Bell, Jill. 1991. *Teaching Multilevel Classes in ESL.* San Diego: Dominie Press.

Although written especially for an ESL setting, offers valuable guidance for teachers of multilevel EFL classes. Appraises the benefits and challenges of multilevel teaching situations. Deals with practical considerations in areas such as curriculum development; activities for whole class, small group, or pair work; and classroom management. Lists resources for activities you can adapt for the multilevel classroom.

*Brown, H. Douglas. 1994. *Teaching by Principles: An Interactive Approach to Language Pedagogy.* Englewood Cliffs, NJ: Prentice Hall, Inc.

Practical, easy-to-read, teaching methodology book. Presents instructional ideas in light of sound theories of second language acquisition. Includes thought-provoking questions for discussion and analysis as well as recommendations for further reading.

*Brown, James Dean. 1995. *The Elements of Language Curriculum: A Systematic Approach to Program Development.* Boston: Heinle & Heinle.

Up-to-date and comprehensive in content. Helps the curriculum developer establish a comprehensive language program; guides the classroom teacher in the formulation of clear teaching objectives. Focuses on needs analysis, goals and objectives, testing, materials, teaching, and program evaluation.

Celce-Murcia, Marianne, Ed. 1991. *Teaching English as a Second or Foreign Language.* 2nd ed. Boston: Heinle & Heinle.

Overview of basic theoretical issues and the many ways theory informs daily instructional choices. Gives insightful background information about ESL/EFL teaching as well as practical applications for each skill area.

Grant, Neville. 1987. *Making the Most of Your Textbook.* New York: Addison-Wesley Longman.

Helps teachers to evaluate and select ESL/EFL teaching materials. Offers practical suggestions for adapting or supplementing current texts.

Larsen-Freeman, Diane. 1986. *Techniques and Principles in Language Teaching.* New York: Oxford University Press.

Using a framework similar to that of Richards and Rogers (see below), presents eight language teaching methods/approaches. Explains the underlying theoretical principles and some of the most common classroom techniques associated with each method.

*Omaggio Hadley, Alice. 1993. *Teaching Language in Context: Proficiency-Oriented Instruction.* 2nd ed. Boston: Heinle & Heinle.

Addresses the needs of teachers of modern foreign languages. Excellent overview of topics such as the nature of language proficiency and the routes adult learners use to develop proficiency in a second language. Includes activities to use with secondary and adult learners as well as a topical bibliography of materials on related topics.

Oxford, Rebecca L. 1990. *Language Learning Strategies: What Every Teacher Should Know.* Boston: Heinle & Heinle.

Based on the premise that language learners can control and improve their own learning, identifies and categorizes a wide range of language learning strategies. Offers numerous practical suggestions for helping learners utilize the strategies presented.

*Richards, Jack and Theodore S. Rodgers. 1986. *Approaches and Methods in Language Teaching: A Description and Analysis.* New York: Cambridge University Press.

Provides a comprehensive and objective analysis of the major approaches and methods used in second language teaching. Each method is discussed separately and is examined from a historical perspective as well as from theoretical and practical viewpoints.

*Richards, Jack C. 1990. *The Language Teaching Matrix: Curriculum, Methodology, and Materials.* New York: Cambridge University Press.

Encourages teachers to investigate effective teaching and learning techniques and to consider the interactive and multidimensional aspects of the language classroom. Focuses on three factors that interact in language teaching: curriculum, methodology, and instructional materials.

Scarcella, Robin C. and Rebecca L. Oxford. 1992. *The Tapestry of Language Learning: The Individual in the Communicative Classroom.* Boston: Heinle & Heinle.

> Establishes the theoretical framework used in the development of the Tapestry series of classroom teaching/learning materials, and defines the "Tapestry Approach" to language teaching and learning. Provides valuable information on factors that affect learning. Examines the teaching of individual language skills and integrated skills.

*Snow, Don. 1996. *More Than a Native Speaker: An Introduction for Volunteers Teaching Abroad.* Alexandria, VA: TESOL, Inc.

> Offers a wealth of highly useful, non-technical advice for new teachers; serves as a refresher course for experienced teachers. Easy-to-read and well-organized, it covers basic principles of language learning and teaching, course planning and individual lesson planning, the teaching of specific language skills and culture, adjustment to a new culture, and opportunities for professional development.

Teaching resources for specific language skills

CHILDREN

*Ashworth, Mary. 1992. *The First Step on the Longer Path: Becoming an ESL Teacher.* Portsmouth, NH: Heinemann.

> Establishes a theoretical foundation for the child's language learning process and provides practical ideas for transferring theory into effective classroom instruction. Written so that the inexperienced teacher can begin to formulate a philosophy of instruction.

Ashworth, Mary and H. Patricia Wakefield. 1994. *Teaching the World's Children: ESL for Ages Three to Seven.* Portsmouth, NH: Heinemann.

> Focuses on practical ways that early childhood and primary educators can help non-English speaking children learn English at a young age. Offers sound advice for building a classroom that invites all children to succeed.

Coelho, Elizabeth. 1994. *Learning Together in the Multicultural Classroom.* Portsmouth, NH: Heinemann.

> Firmly rooted in theories about the importance of cooperative learning, helps classroom teachers to understand the keys to organizing classroom instruction. Provides many practical ideas for group work as well as strategies that enable teachers to generate their own learning activities.

*Piper, Terry. 1993. *And Then There Were Two: Children and Second Language Learning.* Portsmouth, NH: Heinemann.

> Provides answers to many of the basic questions about how children learn a second language and challenges current thinking about the language learning process. An encouraging and stimulating resource for novice and experienced teachers.

Scott, Wendy A. and Lisbeth Ytreberg. 1990. *Teaching English to Children.* New York: Addison-Wesley Longman.

> Offers straightforward advice and insights for teaching children. Presents practical ideas for lessons and activities for the four language skills, as well as affordable supplemental materials that you can create.

COMMUNICATION

Ladousse, Gillian Porter. 1987. *Role Play.* New York: Oxford University Press.

> Equips experienced teachers with fresh ideas to try out in the classroom. For newer teachers, it is an instruction manual complete with detailed background information and suggestions for the effective use of role plays.

Nolasco, Rob and Lois Arthur. 1987. *Conversation*. New York: Oxford University Press.

Provides a brief analysis of some basic features of native-speaker conversation. Helps the teacher to understand some key instructional elements required for the development of conversational fluency. The majority of the book contains a variety of tasks for classroom use.

*Ur, Penny. 1981. *Discussions That Work: Task-Centered Fluency Practice*. New York: Cambridge University Press.

Focuses on the use of class discussions to increase fluency. Offers suggestions for conducting effective discussions. Over 50 examples for learners at various levels.

COMPOSITION

*Leki, Ilona. 1992. *Understanding ESL Writers: A Guide for Teachers*. Portsmouth, NH: Heinemann.

Equips teachers with an understanding of the issues they must work through and the struggles second language writers face. Offers an insightful and careful examination of the writing process, including theoretical background about ESL/EFL writing and models of second language acquisition, an analysis of the diversity that students bring to the writing classroom, and a discussion of practical concerns such as creating writing assignments and grading.

Raimes, Ann. 1983. *Techniques in Teaching Writing*. New York: Oxford University Press.

Offers an array of practical ideas for helping students learn to write. Looks at basic approaches to teaching writing and identifies key questions teachers must answer in order to make decisions about day-to-day teaching practices. Also focuses on different techniques related to teaching the writing process.

CULTURE

*Damen, Louise. 1987. *Culture Learning: The Fifth Dimension in the Language Classroom*. New York: Addison-Wesley Longman.

Helps to bridge the gap between intercultural communication and second or foreign language learning and teaching. Discusses theory and practice related to teaching culture as part of the curriculum.

Weeks, William H., et al. Ed. 1979. *A Manual of Structured Experiences for Cross-Cultural Learning*. Yarmouth, ME: Intercultural Press, Inc.

Provides a variety of group exercises which helps students clarify their own values and communication patterns while learning more about others' beliefs. Each activity is clearly explained with a basic lesson plan. Although it is an older publication, its unique approach works well in some EFL instructional settings.

ENGLISH FOR SPECIFIC PURPOSES

*Hutchinson, Tom and Alan Waters. 1987. *English for Specific Purposes: A Learning-Centred Approach*. New York: Cambridge University Press.

Offers a systematic introduction to this highly specialized area within EFL teaching. Defines ESP within a historical framework, outlines the basic principles of course design and teaching techniques, and examines the role of the teacher. Regardless of the type of ESP course taught, this book provides a strong foundation to build upon.

GRAMMAR

Celce-Murcia, Marianne and Sharon Hilles. 1988. *Techniques and Resources in Teaching Grammar*. New York: Oxford University Press.

Provides a rich understanding of basic issues related to the teaching of grammar. Offers many suggestions and examples for practical activities.

*Ur, Penny. 1988. *Grammar Practice Activities: A Practical Guide for Teachers*. New York: Cambridge University Press.

Presents a collection of creative activities to make grammar teaching more varied and communicative. Offers basic guidelines for instruction. Organized according to grammatical structure, many activities include reproducible charts, grids, or pictures.

LISTENING

Mendelsohn, David J. and Joan Rubin, Eds. 1995. *A Guide for the Teaching of Second Language Listening*. San Diego: Dominie Press.

Presents an in-depth look at research dealing with the theories that inform pedagogy for teaching listening. Also focuses on procedures for teaching listening in the classroom.

Rost, Michael. 1991. *Listening in Action*. Englewood Cliffs, NJ: Prentice Hall, Inc.

Excellent overview of the theoretical issues related to teaching listening. Includes an extensive collection of teaching activities categorized according to type of activity and required student response. Additional annotated resources are listed in the introduction.

Ur, Penny. 1984. *Teaching Listening Comprehension*. New York: Cambridge University Press.

Provides a solid theoretical base to help teachers develop a sound understanding of the types of skills involved in effective listening, the problems that learners experience, and the factors teachers must control when planning a listening curriculum. Offers suggestions and activities for teaching a variety of age and proficiency levels.

PRONUNCIATION

*Avery, Peter and Susan Ehrlich. 1992. *Teaching American English Pronunciation*. New York: Oxford University Press.

Helps teachers to develop an understanding of the technical aspects of English phonology at the sound and phrase levels. Identifies some of the most common pronunciation problems and offers general teaching tips. Includes a variety of techniques and types of instructional activities.

*Celce-Murcia, Marianne, et al. 1996. *Teaching Pronunciation: A Reference for Teachers of English as a Second or Foreign Language*. New York: Cambridge University Press.

Presents the phonological system of North American English at the sound and phrase levels. Discusses key issues in pronunciation instruction and presents a variety of teaching techniques and activities ranging from traditional to communicative.

READING AND LITERATURE

Carter, Ronald and Michael N. Long. 1991. *Teaching Literature*. New York: Addison-Wesley Longman.

Provides a framework and rationale for the use of literature within the EFL curriculum. Includes a focus on classroom procedures and teaching strategies as well as information about how to choose texts appropriate for a particular culture.

Silberstein, Sandra. 1994. *Techniques and Resources in Teaching Reading*. New York: Oxford University Press.

Addresses theoretical and practical issues. Especially useful for inexperienced teachers, offers numerous suggestions for teaching expository prose, nonprose reading, fiction, poetry, and songs. Includes chapter on developing teacher-made materials.

TESTING

Heaton, J. B. 1990. *Classroom Testing.* New York: Addison-Wesley Longman.

Provides a practical look at classroom language testing. Answers many commonly asked questions about testing and also includes some excellent examples of tests that teachers can use or adapt. Each chapter contains an "Activities" section which gives readers an opportunity to evaluate various tests and create their own tests using the guidelines presented.

Hughes, Arthur. 1989. *Testing for Language Teachers.* New York: Cambridge University Press.

Helps classroom teachers to write better tests. Discusses the basic principles of testing and includes a collection of testing techniques. Identifies the stages of test construction, various kinds of testing, and desirable qualities of every test.

*Madsen, Harold S. 1983. *Techniques in Testing.* New York: Oxford University Press.

Contains practical and understandable explanations about test construction and administration. Identifies effective testing possibilities for various skills and subskills. Equips inexperienced and experienced teachers to understand the testing process more clearly and use it as an effective tool to increase learning.

*Underhill, Nic. 1987. *Testing Spoken Language: A Handbook of Oral Testing Techniques.* New York: Cambridge University Press.

Provides a practical step-by-step procedure to help teachers develop tests for spoken language. Discusses a range of test types and the situations for which each is most appropriate. Lists over 50 testing techniques with possible variations and scoring tips.

VOCABULARY

Allen, Virginia French. 1983. *Techniques in Teaching Vocabulary.* New York: Oxford University Press.

Focuses on creative and practical lesson ideas for teaching vocabulary. Answers commonly asked questions about why we should teach vocabulary, what types of words students need the most, and how to help them acquire these words.

Gairns, Ruth and Stuart Redman. 1986. *Working with Words: A Guide to Teaching and Learning Vocabulary.* New York: Cambridge University Press.

Examines some of the underlying principles that should govern vocabulary selection and teaching practices as well as some of the key issues in vocabulary development which often cause problems for learners. Although somewhat more technical than the other resources cited, the "Reader Activities" section helps the teacher think through the concepts in a practical way. Includes sample activities.

Morgan, John and Mario Rinvolucri. 1986. *Vocabulary.* New York: Oxford University Press.

Looks at words as one of the key building blocks of language development. Identifies some of the major issues in vocabulary learning, and presents a variety of learning activities laid out in the form of lesson plans. The activities deal with pre-teaching of vocabulary for reading, building images with words, categorizing words, using dictionaries, and creative ways to review words.

Taylor, Linda L. 1990. *Teaching and Learning Vocabulary.* Englewood Cliffs, NJ: Prentice Hall, Inc.

Focuses on theoretical aspects of vocabulary teaching and provides many real life language examples. Offers practical ideas for teaching vocabulary communicatively, extending the students' general knowledge of words, and working with vocabulary in discourse.

RESOURCE MATERIALS

Clark, Raymond C., et al. 1991. *The ESL Miscellany: An Inventory of American English for Teachers and Students.* 2nd ed. Brattleboro, VT: Pro Lingua Associates.

Contains ready-to-use lists of words and other helpful information for teachers who are writing their own materials. Includes a variety of subject areas, ranging from linguistic and communicative items to culture and nonverbal communication.

Cooper, Richard, et al. 1991. *Video.* New York: Oxford University Press.

Helps teachers find creative ways to utilize the medium of videotape in their classrooms. Explores active viewing and discussion of professional videos as well as class videotaping with the whole class or small groups.

Day, Richard R., Ed. 1993. *New Ways in Teaching Reading.* Alexandria, VA: TESOL, Inc.

Collection of activities, exercises, and suggestions to use in teaching extensive, intensive, and oral reading to all levels of ESL/EFL learners. For each activity, indicates level, aims, required class time, preparation time, and additional resources.

Eby, J. Wesley. 1990. *Handbook for Teaching Bible-Based ESL.* Kansas City, MO: Publications International.

Offers helpful information about ESL/EFL teaching, especially in the area of Bible-based instruction. Includes practical teaching tips for the novice teacher as well as a listing of secular and Christian publishers.

*Nilsen, Don L. F. and Alleen Pace Nilsen. 1973. *Pronunciation Contrasts in English.* Englewood Cliffs, NJ: Prentice Hall, Inc.

Provides a list of sounds that are especially difficult for ESL/EFL learners along with minimal pairs that contain these sounds. Includes facial diagrams, descriptive information about the sounds, and a listing of language groups which typically have difficulty with each contrast. Invaluable resource for pronunciation teaching.

Sadow, Stephen A. 1982. *Idea Bank: Creative Activities for the Language Class.* Boston: Heinle & Heinle.

Forty-five communicative activities that encourage students to think creatively and interact purposefully. Clearly set up with a structured lesson plan, each activity encourages students to take on new roles and become creative problem solvers.

*Ur, Penny and Andrew Wright. 1992. *Five-Minute Activities: A Resource Book of Short Activities.* New York: Cambridge University Press.

Over 100 ideas for quick activities to spice up any class period. Includes activities to introduce or conclude a lesson, to transition between parts of a lesson, to provide extra practice for grammar or vocabulary, or simply to add an element of fun. They require little preparation and can be used with students at all proficiency levels.

*Wright, Andrew, et al. 1984. *Games for Language Learning.* 2nd ed. New York: Cambridge University Press.

A wealth of games geared to all levels of learners and all four skills. Activities are divided into sections according to the type of game. For each game, lists proficiency level, skills utilized, amount of teacher control, and time required.

*Yorkey, Richard. 1985. *Talk-A-Tivities.* New York: Addison-Wesley Longman.

Collection of blackline masters with problem solving activities for pair work. Information gap activities reinforce communication and authentic discourse. A ready-made resource to provide teachers with variety.

Celce-Murcia, Marianne and Diane Larsen-Freeman. 1983. *The Grammar Book: An ESL/EFL Teacher's Course.* Boston: Heinle & Heinle.

Written specifically for teachers, focuses on the most typical grammatical errors of ESL/EFL learners. Covers only selected areas and is not a comprehensive grammar. Although this text contains some practical teaching suggestions to use with learners, it is an advanced reference book with fairly sophisticated and technical explanations.

*Leech, Geoffrey and Jan Svartvik. 1994. *A Communicative Grammar of English.* 2nd ed. New York: Addison-Wesley Longman.

Although written primarily as a reference grammar for advanced ESL/EFL students, it is an excellent resource for teachers who want a well-organized, easy-to-access reference. Focuses heavily on the role of grammar in oral communication and on the range of English structures.

Swan, Michael and Bernard Smith, Eds. 1987. *Learner English: A Teacher's Guide to Interference and Other Problems.* New York: Cambridge University Press.

Provides useful information about a variety of languages, and compares their phonological and grammatical systems to that of English.

Classroom teaching/learning materials

This section provides a variety of student learning materials. Categorized by language focus, they include basal series (all skills integrated into each text) as well as classroom textbooks for one instructional area (Bible-based ESL/EFL, business English, children, composition, grammar, pronunciation) or a combination of these skills. Also included are TOEFL preparation resources and dictionaries. We recommend that you purchase at least some of these materials for your personal library.

With dozens of titles from which to choose, we tried to list those that are widely used in EFL classrooms as well as those that offer unique strengths in a variety of teaching-learning situations. When evaluating these books, keep in mind that many of them have been written for learners in either an ESL or an EFL context, even though they may be more appropriate in one setting or the other. To help you narrow your selection for a specific instructional need, we marked with an asterisk those that merit special consideration. As you examine this list, note the strengths, limitations, and other characteristics of each text, matching what it has to offer with the information you have gathered about your students (language background, proficiency level, needs and goals, and preferred approaches to learning), your instructional objectives, and your personal teaching preferences.

BASAL SERIES

Byrd, Donald R. H., et al. 1994. *Spectrum: A Communicative Course in English.* Englewood Cliffs, NJ: Prentice Hall, Inc.

Six-level series for beginning through advanced learners, used worldwide. Focuses on real-life communication skills. Offers a variety of activities, from controlled to free, which encourage students to develop fluency and accuracy. Also available: workbooks, teacher's editions, audio cassettes, and student placement and evaluation packets.

Nunan, David. 1995. *Atlas: Learning-Centered Communication.* Boston: Heinle & Heinle.

Four-level series for beginning through high-intermediate students, learner-centered and task-based in its approach. The goal of this series is to use integrated tasks to develop active communication skills, so that learners increase in proficiency level and confidence. Each unit contains a variety of topics; speech functions like greeting, describing, agreeing and disagreeing; and grammatical structures. Also available: workbooks, instructor's extended editions, and audio cassettes.

*Richards, Jack C. 1991. *Interchange*. New York: Cambridge University Press.

Widely used multi-level series. Encourages students to engage in authentic communication from the very beginning stages of language learning. Integrates all four skills and provides meaningful practice activities. Introductory level for true beginners and three additional levels, high-beginning through high-intermediate. Also available: teacher's manuals, workbooks, audio cassettes, and lab cassettes/guides.

BIBLE-BASED ESL/EFL

*International Network. *Adventures in English*. Deerfield, IL: Evangelical Free Church Mission.

Thematically organized materials designed especially for two-week English camps. The *Starter* teacher's manual contains a variety of resources for zero beginners; the *Multi-Level* teacher's manual contains a wealth of activities to make classes interesting and active. One of the strengths is that the Bible lesson is separate but related to the theme of the day, allowing more flexibility when planning the curriculum. Other components are a student journal, Bible study guide, and Bible in simplified English.

Ledyard, Gleason H., translator. 1986. *New Life Study Testament*. Canby, OR: Christian Literature International.

New Testament in simplified English, based on 850-word reading vocabulary. Provides lower-level students with a fairly readable text. Perhaps one drawback is that the use of a very limited vocabulary obscures the meaning of some passages.

BUSINESS ENGLISH

*England, Lizabeth and Christine Uber Grosse. 1995. *Speaking of Business*. Boston: Heinle & Heinle.

Focuses on effective communication strategies in the workplace. Covers specific language and inter-personal skills related to business communication. Authentic tasks offer opportunities for practice in a simulated real-life setting. From the *Tapestry* series.

Vetrano, Joni, et al. 1995. *Let's Talk Business*. Boston: Heinle & Heinle.

Advanced business communication text designed to prepare students for academic study in business-related fields. Provides an integrated approach which allows learners to focus on written and verbal business communication. Offers cultural information about the corporate world and typical interaction situations. From the *Tapestry* series.

CHILDREN

Schimpff, Jill Wagner. 1982. *Open Sesame Picture Dictionary*. New York: Oxford University Press.

Presents over 550 high-frequency vocabulary words with colorful illustrations. Familiar Sesame Street characters make learning fun and interesting. Vocabulary items are presented in context and individually. Also available: activity book.

Walker, Michael. 1992. *Addison Wesley ESL*. New York: Addison-Wesley Longman.

Five-level children's series presents academic and social language as well as some content instruction in math, science, and social studies. Books are colorful and inviting. Teacher's edition gives many ideas for introducing and practicing language skills. Also available: workbooks, audio cassettes, big books, testing packages, and other resources.

COMPOSITION

Arnaudet, Martin L. and Mary Ellen Barrett. 1990. *Paragraph Development: A Guide for Students of English as a Second Language*. 2nd ed. Englewood Cliffs, NJ: Prentice Hall, Inc.

Intermediate to high-intermediate text provides a fairly structured approach to teaching composition from the sentence level through paragraphs. Helps students to understand the basic elements of writing and the major rhetorical patterns in English.

*Blanchard, Karen and Christine Root. 1994. *Ready to Write: A First Composition Text.* 2nd ed. New York: Addison-Wesley Longman.

High-beginning to low-intermediate text clearly presents the writing process. Explains the basic components of a strong composition; provides practice with several of the major organizational patterns used in English. Its use of real life situations as a context for writing gives students an authentic purpose to motivate their work.

*Ingram, Beverly and Carol King. 1988. *From Writing to Composing: An Introductory Composition Course for Students of English.* New York: Cambridge University Press.

Helps beginning to low-intermediate students work creatively through the writing process by weaving together structured writing activities with free composing. Encourages verbal interaction in the pre-writing steps, which in turn helps students generate ideas for writing. Teacher's manual provides teaching guidelines and additional exercises and is an essential component of the course.

Kadesch, Margot C. et al. 1991. *Insights into Academic Writing: Strategies for Advanced Students.* New York: Addison-Wesley Longman.

Encourages students to draw on their own knowledge base as well as that acquired through reading and discussion in order to develop interesting essays. For advanced students, focuses on academic writing suitable for the college level. Each unit contains pre-writing activities as well as instruction on areas such as thesis writing, topic sentences, and using quotations for support.

Reid, Joy M. 1996. *Basic Writing.* 2nd ed. Englewood Cliffs, NJ: Prentice Hall, Inc.

Beginning-level text for students with a limited proficiency in English and who need to focus on more experiential, non-academic writing. Student paragraphs written at a variety of skill levels introduce vocabulary and sentence structure that learners can use to compose their own paragraphs on similar topics. Some assignments encourage interaction with classmates to build communicative competence and foster new ideas.

Reid, Joy M. 1988. *The Process of Composition.* 2nd ed. Englewood Cliffs, NJ: Prentice Hall, Inc.

Advanced level text leads students through increasingly complex writing tasks, starting with the paragraph, then moving to the essay, and finishing with the research paper. Provides an overall framework and then helps learners practice and refine their skills.

*Reid, Joy M. and Margaret Lindstrom. 1994. *The Process of Paragraph Writing.* 2nd ed. Englewood Cliffs, NJ: Prentice Hall, Inc.

Focused on the paragraph level, this text gives intermediate students a basis for understanding academic writing from the decision-making aspects about audience and topic through the pre-writing and actual writing stages. Contains examples of student writing and sequenced assignments that build the learners' skills.

*Wong, Rita, et al. 1987. *Becoming a Writer: Developing Academic Writing Skills.* New York: Addison-Wesley Longman.

Preceded by *Ready to Write* (see above), helps high-intermediate students develop their writing skills from the beginning stages of creating and gathering their ideas to the final stages of revision. Contains interesting information to stimulate thinking as well as practical information about the rhetorical issues of audience and basic organization as well as grammatical structures. Students are then asked to apply this knowledge by writing on a related topic.

GRAMMAR

*Azar, Betty Schrampfer. *Azar Grammar Series.* Englewood Cliffs, NJ: Prentice Hall, Inc.

> *Basic English Grammar.* 2nd ed. 1996. (beginning to high-beginning)
> *Fundamentals of English Grammar.* 2nd ed. 1992. (intermediate)
> *Understanding and Using English Grammar.* 2nd ed. 1989. (high-intermediate to advanced)
> *Chartbook.* 1993. (charts from *Fundamentals of English Grammar* and *Understanding and Using English Grammar*)

> Popular series characterized by clear explanations and numerous written and oral practice activities. Although these texts are not as contextualized as many on the market, they continue to be widely used as teaching texts and also as references for teachers. Also available (for all texts except *Chartbook*): teacher's guides, workbooks, and answer keys.

*Breyer, Pamela Peterson. 1995, 1996. *Grammarwork.* 2nd ed. Englewood Cliffs, NJ: Prentice Hall, Inc.

> *Book 1* (beginning), *Book 2* (high-beginning), *Book 3* (intermediate), *Book 4* (high-intermediate)

> Series of four workbooks provides useful practice on a variety of grammar topics. Each grammar point is explained concisely, and the contextualized exercises use practical language. Ideal as a supplemental resource for individual or classroom practice.

Deakins, Alice H., et al. 1994. *The Tapestry Grammar: A Reference for Learners of English.* Boston: Heinle & Heinle.

> Excellent reference for teachers and advanced learners. Contains clear and concise explanations of rules along with meaningful, contextualized examples. Current in its content. Accounts for informal and formal language in spoken and written form.

*Larsen-Freeman, Diane. Series Ed. 1993. *Grammar Dimensions: Form, Meaning, and Use.* Boston: Heinle & Heinle.

> Popular grammar series is rich in content and up-to-date in its contextualized practice. With four levels ranging from beginning to advanced, accompanying workbooks, and split editions for shorter courses, it is very adaptable to a variety of teaching situations. For each grammatical point, learners practice the form, the meaning, and the use of the structure in communication.

Jones, Leo. 1992. *Communicative Grammar Practice: Activities for Intermediate Students of English.* New York: Cambridge University Press.

> Provides a wealth of creative ideas to help intermediate to advanced students practice grammatical structures in conversational English. Includes grammar summaries, exercises for pairs or groups, and information gap activities. Helps to bridge the gap between form and meaning.

Laporte, Penny and Jay Maurer. 1985. *Structure Practice in Context: Books 1, 2, & 3.* New York: Addison-Wesley Longman.

> *Book 1* (beginning), *Book 2* (intermediate), *Book 3* (high-intermediate)

> Series provides one to two pages of contextualized, communicative activities for each grammar topic. Excellent resource for supplemental practice exercises.

*McKay, Irene, et al. 1996. *Tapestry Grammar Strands, Books 1-5.* Boston: Heinle & Heinle.

> Five-book series combines grammar and communication practice for beginning through advanced levels. Books 1-2 (beginning and low-intermediate) provide more explanation than do Books 3-5 (intermediate-high, advanced-low, and advanced-high), which are more like workbooks to be used in conjunction with other materials.

*Murphy, Raymond. 1989. *Grammar in Use: Reference and Practice for Intermediate Students of English*. New York: Cambridge University Press.

Unique combination of reference grammar and practice book. Useful for classroom use or self study. Presents manageable segments of grammar and includes two-page units about each topic. Also available: separate answer key.

Rinvolucri, Mario. 1984. *Grammar Games: A Resource Book for Teachers*. New York: Cambridge University Press.

Excellent resource to spice up grammar instruction. Contains competitive and collaborative games, as well as more interpersonal and drama-oriented activities. Some activities are more British than American.

*Schoenberg, Irene (basic) and Marjorie Fuchs (intermediate) and Jay Maurer (advanced). 1994, 1995. *Focus on Grammar*. New York: Addison-Wesley Longman.

Series includes a clear presentation of grammar points with communicative exercises. Many of the activities require pair work. Also available: workbooks, audio cassettes, and teacher's guides with diagnostic and final tests.

ORAL COMMUNICATION (LISTENING/SPEAKING AND CONVERSATION)

*Byrd, Donald R. H. and Isis Clemente-Cabetas. 1991. *React-Interact: Situations for Communication*. 2nd ed. Englewood Cliffs, NJ: Prentice Hall, Inc.

Encourages intermediate to advanced students to expand their knowledge of vocabulary and grammar through actual communication in which they discuss a variety of topics and share their opinions. Popular in ESL conversation classes, but it could be adapted or used as a supplemental text in EFL classes in which the book's designated discussion topics are culturally appropriate.

Genzel, Rhona B. and Martha Graves Cummings. 1994. *Culturally Speaking: A Conversation and Culture Text*. 2nd ed. Boston: Heinle & Heinle.

For intermediate level and above, helps learners to speak and act comfortably in an ESL context by comparing their own cultural behaviors and norms with those of North Americans. Although this book is much more ESL oriented because of its many out-of-class activities designed to explore the new culture, it has some useful lessons on nonverbal communication and gestures as well as situational language.

Gill, Mary Mc Vey and Pamela Hartmann. 1993. *Get It? Got It!: Listening to Others; Speaking for Ourselves*. Boston: Heinle & Heinle.

Provides low-intermediate students with a bridge from basic survival skills to more advanced conversational techniques. Primary emphasis on listening and speaking, but some focus on reading and writing. Offers many opportunities for interactive group and pair work. Part of the *Tapestry* series.

James, Gary. 1993. *Passages: Exploring Spoken English*. Boston: Heinle & Heinle.

Helps high-intermediate students to develop effective listening strategies. Contains authentic oral language from conversations, news broadcasts, lectures, and advertisements. Activities for pair practice, discussion, and working with authentic written sources such as newspapers and magazines. Part of the *Tapestry* series.

Jones, Leo and C. von Baeyer. 1983. *Functions of American English: Communication Activities for the Classroom*. New York: Cambridge University Press.

For high-intermediate to advanced students, focuses on language functions such as greeting, agreeing and disagreeing, and giving advice. Encourages students to think about sociolinguistic concerns such as setting, role of participants, and level of formality. Each chapter includes a sample dialogue demonstrating a language function, a presentation of key phrases and other relevant information, and communication exercises.

*Levine, Deena R., et al. 1987. *The Culture Puzzle: Cross-Cultural Communication for ESL.* Englewood Cliffs, NJ: Prentice Hall, Inc.

Helps intermediate to advanced learners integrate language and culture learning. Provides practice with several key strategies that can help students become more confident, active communicators. Contains cultural information about the United States as well as "culture puzzles" for the students to work through.

Rooks, George. 1990. *Can't Stop Talking.* 2nd ed. Boston: Heinle & Heinle.

Constructed much like *React-Interact* (see above), offers high-beginning to low-intermediate students an opportunity to discuss a variety of topics and share their opinions in small groups. Can be adapted as a primary text or used as a supplemental resource for classes in which the book's designated conversation topics are culturally appropriate.

Rooks, George. 1988. *The Non-Stop Discussion Workbook.* 2nd ed. Boston: Heinle & Heinle.

Provides intermediate to advanced students with a structured approach to discussion by offering a variety of situations to stimulate ideas and interaction. Units are divided into five basic parts: read, consider, decide and write, discuss, and extend.

*Rost, Michael. 1994. *Prime Time English.* New York: Addison-Wesley Longman. (Also available: teacher's manual and audio cassettes.)

*Rost, Michael. 1994. *Real Time English.* New York: Addison-Wesley Longman. (Also available: teacher's manual and audio cassettes.)

*Rost, Michael and Angela Blackwell. 1995. *Future Time English.* New York: Addison-Wesley Longman. (Also available: student workbook.)

Three-book series offers an interesting and carefully planned listening and speaking curriculum for beginning to low-intermediate students with practical activities relevant to real life. Using a variety of oral activities including information gap, each book focuses on spoken communication while building grammar and vocabulary.

*Tillitt, Bruce and Mary Newton Bruder. 1985. *Speaking Naturally: Communication Skills in American English.* New York: Cambridge University Press.

Focuses on speech acts or language functions such as invitations, apologies, agreeing and disagreeing. Helps students to understand and use the social rules of language. Employing a fairly structured approach, each unit contains model dialogues with discussion questions, a reading about the language function, a list of some commonly used phrases, and small group or pair practice and role play ideas.

Pronunciation

Baker, Ann and Sharon Goldstein. 1990. *Pronunciation Pairs: An Introductory Course for Students of English.* New York: Cambridge University Press.

For beginning-level students, focuses on the vowels and consonants of English, although some of the exercises touch on intonation and stress. A unique aspect of the book is its use of pictures, which makes learning more fun and accessible for beginning-level students. Also available: teacher's manual and audio cassettes.

*Beisbier, Beverly. 1994, 1995. *Sounds Great.* Boston: Heinle & Heinle. *Book 1* (1994, beginning), *Book 2* (1995, intermediate).

Offers an interesting and well-balanced approach to teaching pronunciation for high-beginning through intermediate levels. Helps students discover the rules for the English stress and intonation system. Includes practice exercises for listening and production; provides a range of activities from controlled to communicative for the sound level, word level, and phrase level. Also available: teacher's manuals and audio cassettes.

Dauer, Rebecca M. 1993. *Accurate English: A Complete Course in Pronunciation.* Englewood Cliffs, NJ: Prentice Hall, Inc.

For high-intermediate to advanced students, focuses on the sounds, rhythm, and intonation of English. Includes stress patterns for words and phrases, some typical spelling patterns, and rules for stress placement.

*Gilbert, Judy B. 1993. *Clear Speech.* 2nd ed. New York: Cambridge University Press.

For intermediate to advanced students, focuses on the "musical" aspects of English—rhythm, stress, and intonation. Individual and paired practice activities encourage students to improve their production and comprehension skills. Also available: teacher's book and audio cassettes.

*Graham, Carolyn. 1978. *Jazz Chants.* New York: Oxford University Press.

Popular with teachers and their students for many years, these fun-to-do chants give beginning through advanced students practice with the rhythmic expression of English. Each jazz chant focuses on different elements of phrase level rhythm and intonation as well as reduced speech. Includes teaching notes.

Other jazz chant books by Carolyn Graham: *Grammar Chants.* 1993; *Small Talk: More Jazz Chants.* 1986; *Jazz Chants for Children.* 1979; *Mother Goose Jazz Chants.* 1994.

Weinstein, Nina. 1982. *Whaddaya Say?* Englewood Cliffs, NJ: Prentice Hall, Inc.

Explores the area of reduced speech forms or fast speech phenomena and the typical linking, trimming, and blending that occurs in what this book calls "relaxed speech." Allows students to hear relaxed pronunciation versus careful pronunciation and to associate the actual spelling of words with their pronunciation in casual conversation. Also available: audio cassette.

TOEFL PREPARATION RESOURCES

*Gear, Jolene. 1993. *Cambridge Preparation for the TOEFL Test.* New York: Cambridge University Press.

Prepares students for the TOEFL Test through a series of practice activities which build language and test-taking skills. Includes nearly five hours of listening material on cassette. To help students gauge their progress and predict their score, two complete TOEFL-format practice tests are included. An answer key explains why answers are correct or incorrect.

OTHER RESOURCES: DICTIONARIES

ENGLISH-ENGLISH

Longman Dictionary of American English. 1983. New York: Addison-Wesley Longman.

For intermediate to advanced learners, offers several unique features which make the information accessible: definitions use a restricted vocabulary of 2,000 words; idioms are clearly marked and included after the main entries; signposts help students to quickly locate the correct definition. Also available: a workbook which helps students learn how to use the dictionary more effectively.

Longman Dictionary of English Idioms. 1979. New York: Addison-Wesley Longman.

Identifies 5,000 idioms. Uses a restricted vocabulary of 2,000 words. Excellent reference tool for current colloquial language.

McArthur, Tom. *Longman Lexicon of Contemporary English.* 1981. New York: Addison-Wesley Longman.

Helps students to understand the complexities of related words by categorizing them into 14 semantic areas related to daily use. Through definitions and examples, students learn the subtle differences between related words.

The Newbury House Dictionary of American English. 1996. Boston: Heinle & Heinle.

Offers straightforward definitions with sample sentences. Includes a wide variety of idioms, phrasal verbs, and current business and technology jargon. "Challenge synonyms" help students to improve their vocabulary by introducing them to less frequently used synonyms for common words.

PICTURE DICTIONARIES

*Molinsky, Steven J. and Bill Bliss. 1994. *Word by Word Picture Dictionary*. Englewood Cliffs, NJ: Prentice Hall, Inc.

More than a picture dictionary; this program enables students to learn vocabulary while practicing words and phrases in meaningful contexts. In addition to colorful pictures with vocabulary listed below, simple dialogues provide further practice. Bilingual editions are available for Spanish, Japanese, Chinese, Korean, Portuguese, Vietnamese, Russian, and Haitian Kreyol. Also available: workbook; teacher's resource book; audio cassettes; and visual aids such as charts, transparencies, and game cards.

Parnwell, E. C. 1988. *The New Oxford Picture Dictionary*. New York: Oxford University Press.

Over 2,400 vocabulary items organized and presented thematically with colorful illustrations. Bilingual editions are available for Cambodian, Chinese, Japanese, Korean, Navajo, Polish, Russian, Spanish, and Vietnamese. Also available: teacher's guide and workbooks.

*Rosenthal, Marilyn S. and Daniel B. Freeman. 1987. *Longman Photo Dictionary*. New York: Addison-Wesley Longman.

Introduces over 2,000 vocabulary items. Teacher's guide offers suggestions for activities to enhance language development. Bilingual editions are available for Spanish, Chinese, Japanese, and Korean. Also available: workbooks and audio cassettes.

PUBLISHERS AND DISTRIBUTORS

This section provides contact information for a variety of publishers and distributors of secular and Christian EFL materials, including the publishers of all books cited in this chapter. By listing a publisher, we do not imply that we recommend or endorse all books by that publisher. Whether secular or Christian, materials vary considerably in quality and focus. They should be selected with a particular teaching-learning situation in mind. For example, if your primary purpose is to teach English, rather than conduct Bible studies or devotionals, your materials should place the major emphasis on the teaching of EFL, not on the biblical content. The guidelines discussed earlier in this chapter can help you make appropriate choices.

Secular publishers and distributors

In most major cities, you can find one or more bookstores that carry materials for teachers and learners of EFL. They frequently display a variety of items by major publishers such as Cambridge University Press, Addison-Wesley Longman, Oxford University Press, and Prentice Hall International. If a book you want is not in stock, they may be able to order it.

You can also purchase books directly from the publisher or from a distributor of EFL materials. Below you will find the telephone and fax numbers and mailing addresses of the major secular publishers of professional resources and classroom teaching/learning materials, as well as the two largest TESL/TEFL distributors in the United States (marked with an asterisk). We encourage you to use this contact information to order free catalogs. These usually contain a brief description, ISBN number, and price for each item; ordering information; and often a list of overseas branches of the company.

Although procedures often change over time, some companies have rather strict policies concerning book orders from individuals not associated directly with an educational institution. For example, discounts are sometimes given only to those who use the institution's name when ordering, and examination copies may not be available to those working outside the typical educational setting. Shipping and handling fees also vary with the publisher.

Addison-Wesley Longman
Order Services
1 Jacob Way
Reading, MA 01867-9984
(800) 552-2259 (K - 12 schools)
(800) 322-1377 (college and
   adults)
(800) 333-3328 (fax)

United Kingdom:
Sales Department, ELT Division
Edinburgh Gate
Burnt Mill
Harlow, Essex CM20 2JE
United Kingdom
+44 (0) 1279-623623
+44 (0) 1279-623947 (fax)

*Alta ESL Resource Center
14 Adrian Court
Burlingame, CA 94010
(800) ALTA/ESL
(800) ALTA/FAX (fax)

Cambridge University Press
Order Fulfillment
110 Midland Ave.
Port Chester, NY 10573-4930
(800) 872-7423
(914) 937-4712 (fax)

Canada:
Pippin Publishing Ltd.
(address below)

United Kingdom:
ELT Marketing Department
The Edinburgh Building
Shaftsbury Road
Cambridge CB2 2RU
England
(0223) 312393
(0223) 315052 (fax)

*Delta Systems
1400 Miller Parkway
McHenry, IL 60050-7030
(800) 323-8270
(800) 909-9901 (fax)

Dominie Press
5945 Pacific Center Blvd.
Suite 505
San Diego, CA 92121
(800) 232-4570
(619) 546-8822 (fax)

Edward Arnold
Routledge, Chapman & Hall
(distributor)
29 West 35th Street
New York, NY 10001
(800) 634-7064
(800) 248-4724 (fax)

Harcourt Brace & Co.
4th Floor
6277 Sea Harbor Dr.
Orlando, FL 32887
(800) 742-5375 (information)
(800) 225-5425 (orders)
(800) 874-6418 (fax)

Heinemann
361 Hanover Street
Portsmouth, NH 03801-3912
(800) 541-2086
(800) 847-0938 (fax)

Heinle & Heinle
ITP Distribution Center
7625 Empire Dr.
Florence, KY 41042
(800) 354-9706
(606) 525-0978 (fax)

Canada:
Thomas Nelson Canada
1120 Birchmount Rd.
Scarborough, ON M1K 5G4
Canada

United Kingdom:
Nelson ELT
Berkshire House
168-173 High Hollbourn
London WC1 V7AA
United Kingdom
44 71 4971422
44 71 4971426 (fax)

Intercultural Press, Inc.
P.O. Box 700
Yarmouth, ME 04096
(800) 370-2665
(207) 846-5181 (fax)

NTC Publishing Group
4255 West Touhy Ave.
Lincolnwood, IL 60646-1975
(800) 323-4900
(847) 679-2494

Oxford University Press
Order Department
2001 Evans Rd.
Cary, NC 27513
(800) 451-7556
(919) 677-1303 (fax)

United Kingdom:
Oxford University Press
ELT Sales Department
Walton St.
Oxford OX2 6DP
United Kingdom

Pippin Publishing Ltd.
380 Esna Park Drive
Markham, ON L3R 1H5
Canada
(800) 567-6591
(416) 513-6977 (fax)

Prentice Hall, Inc.
Order Processing Dept.
P.O. Box 11073
Des Moines, IA 50336-1073
(800) 947-7700 (single copy orders)
(800) 223-1360 (multiple copy orders)
(515) 284-2607 (fax)

Pro Lingua Associates
15 Elm Street
Brattleboro, VT 05301
(800) 366-4775
(802) 257-5117 (fax)

TESOL
Publications Department
1600 Cameron St., Suite 300
Alexandria, VA 22314-2751
(703) 836-0774
(703) 518-2535 (fax)

The University of Michigan Press
P.O. Box 1104
Ann Arbor, MI 48106-1104
(313) 764-4392
(800) 876-1922 (fax)

Christian publishers and distributors

This section lists Christian companies and organizations from which you can purchase materials for EFL learners. Some publications combine Bible study with the learning of English. Others, such as Bibles in simplified English, are resources you can use with students whose English skills are limited. To get acquainted with the offerings of each company, ask for a free catalog and information about placing orders. For a more complete listing of Bible-based materials, contact CETESOL (see Chapter 5).

Christian Literature International
P.O. Box 777
Canby, OR 97013

International Network/Evangelical Free Church Mission
2065 Half Day Road
Deerfield, IL 60015
(847) 317-8190 (x4181, Outreach English Camps)

Literacy & Evangelism International
1800 S. Jackson
Tulsa, OK 74107
(918) 585-3826
(918) 585-3224 (fax)

Publications International
6401 The Paseo
Kansas City, MO 64131
(800) 462-8711

5. Other Resources

Teachers often ask questions such as these: Which journals can help me to become a better teacher? Are there professional associations that I should join? How do Christian EFL teachers network with one another? What's available on the Internet? Where can I find more information about living overseas? This chapter deals with resources not included elsewhere in this handbook. Some resources inform you about the latest developments in the profession or offer guidance for classroom instruction; others connect you with hundreds of EFL colleagues worldwide; still others tell you what you need to know to move to the country of your choice.

Professional journals

English Teaching Forum. Published quarterly by the United States Information Agency (USIA) for teachers of English outside the United States, this journal focuses on practical concerns of classroom practitioners. For subscription information, contact the Cultural Office of the United States embassy of the capital city in the country in which you reside. Subscriptions in the United States and Canada are available from *English Teaching Forum*, 301 4th Street SW, Room 312, Washington, D.C. 20547. Most articles from recent issues are also available on the World Wide Web. (See the entry for the USIA in the section below on the World Wide Web.)

TESOL Quarterly. Published quarterly by TESOL, this journal focuses on practical applications of theory and research for the teaching of ESL/EFL. In addition to scholarly articles, it includes the following sections: commentary on current trends and practices, discussion of teaching issues, reviews of classroom materials and professional books, and brief reports of research in progress. Subscriptions available to TESOL members only. (See the entry for TESOL in the next section.)

TESOL Journal. Published quarterly by TESOL, this journal contains practical articles of interest to classroom ESL/EFL teachers, teaching tips, reader responses, and reviews of instructional materials and professional books. Subscriptions available to TESOL members only. (See the entry for TESOL in the next section.)

English Language Teaching Journal (ELT). Published quarterly by Oxford University Press in association with the British Council, *ELT* contains practical articles for EFL teachers and administrators. To subscribe, write *ELT Journal*, 2 Smyrna Road, London NW6 4LU, United Kingdom, or call Oxford University Press at (800) 542-2442.

For the two electronic journals, *Internet TESL Journal* and *TESL-EJ*, see the section on the World Wide Web (below).

Professional associations

Teaching English to Speakers of Other Languages (TESOL). Founded in 1966, TESOL's more than 18,000 members worldwide include teachers, teachers-in-training, teacher-preparation specialists, administrators, researchers, materials writers, and curriculum developers. As an international association, TESOL's mission is to strengthen the effective teaching and learning of English as an additional language while respecting individuals' native language rights. Within the organization, there are 19 special interest groups (e.g., English as a Foreign Language, English for Specific Purposes, Teacher Education). TESOL publishes a wide range of professional books and materials as well as three serial publications: *TESOL Quarterly*, *TESOL Journal*, and *TESOL Matters* (a bi-monthly newspaper that highlights professional interests, conferences, and Association news). For its members, TESOL also sponsors a placement service and a bimonthly *TESOL Placement Bulletin*. The annual International TESOL Conference attracts thousands of participants. TESOL, 1600 Cameron Street, Suite 300, Alexandria, VA 22314 USA. Telephone: (703) 836-0774; Fax: (703) 836-6447; E-mail: tesol@tesol.edu.

In addition, there are 88 organizations affiliated with TESOL, representing another 40,000 members. While many of these are state affiliates (e.g., Michigan TESOL, New York State TESOL) others are country affiliates (e.g., Japan TESOL, Argentina TESOL). Most affiliates have their own conferences or cooperate in sponsoring regional conferences.

International Association of Teachers of English as a Foreign Language (IATEFL) is an international organization whose members are largely from countries other than the United States. IATEFL has established branches and affiliated professional organizations worldwide in more than 50 countries. It sponsors an annual international conference and publishes a range of professional materials including the *IATEFL Newsletter* and the newsletters of the 14 special interest groups. For membership information, contact IATEFL, 3 Kingsdown Chambers, Kingsdown Park, Tankerton, Whitstable, Kent, CT5 2DJ, United Kingdom. In addition, see the IATEFL listing on the World Wide Web (http://www.man.ac.uk/IATEFL/) or e-mail the organization (100070.1327@Compuserve.com).

CETESOL (Christian Educators in TESOL) serves as a clearinghouse for information of interest to Christian ESL/EFL teachers. It also publishes a newsletter, holds meetings at the International TESOL Conference, and sponsors an e-mail list, CTESL-L (see entry below). To receive the newsletter, either e-mail the editor, Joan Dungey (DUNGEYJ@cedarnet.cedarville.edu) or write her at 126 N. Walnut Street, Yellow Springs, OH 45387.

World Wide Web

You can find a wealth of useful EFL information on the World Wide Web. This includes journals, newsletters, conference schedules, overseas teaching and learning opportunities, locations to place your resume, lesson plans and teaching materials, resources for specific countries, grants and fellowships, and publishers' catalogs. We have included a few of the key Web resources below; however, new sites are added almost daily. Most of these listings include "links" which allow you to connect to other sites by clicking on an icon, word, or phrase. If you are new to the Web, we suggest you begin with *Linguistic Funland's TESL Page* or *Dave's ESL Cafe.*

English Teaching Forum: http://www.usia.gov/education/engteaching/eal-foru.htm

   Includes most articles from recent issues (see the section on professional journals).

Internet TESL Journal: http://www.aitech.ac.jp/~iteslj/

   For classroom teachers and tutors, this journal includes articles and research papers, lessons and lesson plans, teaching techniques, handouts and other classroom materials, highlights from previous issues, as well as links of interest to EFL teachers and students.

TESL-EJ (Teaching English as a Second or Foreign Language: An Electronic Journal):
   http://violet.berkeley.edu/~cwp/TESL-EJ/

   Contains articles, book reviews, and forum discussions about ESL/EFL teaching practices and second language acquisition.

Linguistic Funland's TESL Page: Resources for teachers and students of English:
   http://math.unr.edu/linguistics/tesl.html

   Offers a wide range of links to other Web sites: Job Opportunities in TESL; Exercises/Activities for ESL Students; Articles and Essays of Interest; Electronic Discussion Groups; E-Mail Pen-Pal Opportunities; Organizations and Journals; ESL Programs and Teacher Training; Fun, Interesting, and Cultural Sites; Miscellaneous Resources; Search Engines and Other Information; Materials and Software; ESL Student Projects; Grant Information; E-Mail the Maintainer; TOEFL and Other Testing Information.

Dave's ESL Cafe: http://www.pacificnet.net/~sperling/eslcafe.html

Offers multiple categories of information for EFL teachers, students and administrators: ESL Job Center; ESL Idiom Page; ESL Quote Page; One-Step ESL Search Page; ESL Quiz Center; ESL Help Center; ESL Idea Page; ESL Graffiti Wall; ESL Question Page; ESL Links for Students; ESL Links for Teachers; ESL Message Exchange; Teacher E-mail Connection; Student E-mail Connection.

ESOL International: A Resource and Information Service for Students and Teachers of English for Speakers of Other Languages: http://www.edunet.com/esol-idx.html

A broad selection of information for EFL students, teachers and administrators: International English Language Schools; The ESOL Job Centre; Education Agents and Student Placement Organizations; Language Exhibitions and Fairs Internationally; English Grammar On-Line; ESOL Administrators Section; English Language Learning Resources for Teachers; English Language Learning Resources for Students; ESOL News.

The United States Information Agency (USIA): http://www.usia.gov/education/engteaching/eal-ndx.htm

In addition to articles from back issues of the *English Teaching Forum* (see the section on Journals), this Web site includes a list of binational centers, teaching opportunities abroad, exchange programs, resources for specific countries, teaching materials, EFL publishers' catalogs, and links to other sites of interest to EFL teachers.

Electronic mail lists

TESL-L (Teachers of English as a Second Language Electronic List). With more than 15,000 participants in over 100 countries, *TESL-L* is the most popular e-mail discussion list for ESL/EFL professionals. *TESL-L* not only serves as a vehicle for on-line discussions, but it also has archives of professional articles and teaching materials which can be downloaded through your computer. To subscribe to the list, send the following e-mail message:

Address:	LISTSERV@CUNYVM.CUNY.EDU
Message:	SUB TESL-L first-name last-name

There are a number of special interest branches or sub-lists of *TESL-L* that are open to all *TESL-L* members. These include sub-lists for the following topics: Technology, Computers and TESL (*TESLCA-L*); Materials Writers (*TESLMW-L*); English for Specific Purposes (*TESP-L*); Teaching English to Children (*TESLK-12*); and Job, Employment and Working Conditions in TESL/TEFL (*TESLJB-L*). When you join *TESL-L*, you receive a listing of all current sub-lists. You can also find a description of *TESL-L* and the sub-lists on the World Wide Web (http://math.unr.edu/linguistics/tesl.html).

CTESL-L (Christian Educators in TESOL List) is a small list that provides a forum in which Christians discuss issues such as a teaching concerns, job openings in Christian institutions, living overseas, etc. To subscribe to the list, send the following e-mail message:

Address:	MAJORDOM@iclnet93.iclnet.org
Message:	SUB CTESL-L first-name last-name

Living and teaching overseas

To learn more about what it's like to live overseas, and to learn a new culture and language, you may want to consult the resources listed below. Each focuses on one or more countries or areas of the world.

Teaching English Overseas: An Introduction, by Sandra Lee McKay (1992, Oxford University Press), addresses teaching situations in a variety of countries. She uses case studies to discuss the impact each of the following has on EFL teaching: sociopolitical factors (Cameroon, Malaysia, the Philippines), economic conditions (Thailand, the Philippines), cultural context (Saudi Arabia, Japan), language education policies (Malaysia, the Philippines, Japan), and institutional structures (Turkey, Tanzania, Spain, Japan).

Teaching English in Eastern and Central Europe by Robert Lynes (1996, NTC Publishing Group) offers a wealth of practical advice for teaching English in Poland (60 pages), the Czech Republic (63 pages), Slovakia (20 pages), Hungary (65 pages), and Bulgaria (11 pages). For each country, the author discusses how to prepare for living and teaching overseas, find a teaching position, and manage daily living concerns while teaching English.

Teaching English in Japan by Jerry O'Sullivan (1996, NTC Publishing Group) offers practical advice on finding a teaching position as well as living and teaching in Japan.

Teach English in Japan by Charles Wordell and Greta Gorsuch, Eds. (1992, *The Japan Times*, distributed by TESOL) is a reference guide that helps native English speakers understand and handle appropriately their professional and personal problems related to teaching English while living in Japan.

NCELTR (National Centre for English Language Teaching and Research) publishes a highly popular series of texts, each focusing on the language and culture of a specific country. Some of the texts include chapters on topics such as religion and social life. Their address is listed at the end of this chapter. You can also reach them through e-mail (sales@nceltr.nceltr.mq.edu.au) or the World Wide Web (http://www.nceltr.mq.edu.au). This series is distributed in the United States by Alta ESL Resource Center (address at the end of Chapter 4).

> *China: A Handbook in Intercultural Communication.* (Jean Brick, 1991)
> *Japan: A Handbook in Intercultural Communication.* (Tomoko Koyama, 1992)
> *Lebanon: A Handbook in Intercultural Communication.* (Peter Clark and Robin Thelwell, 1996)
> *Poland: A Handbook in Intercultural Communication.* (Eddie Ronowicz, 1995)
> *Thailand: A Handbook in Intercultural Communication.* (Kerry O'Sullivan and Songphorn Tajaroensuk, 1996)

Two additional titles are forthcoming:

> *Indonesia: A Handbook in Intercultural Communication.*
> *Vietnam: A Handbook in Intercultural Communication.*

Intercultural Press offers a wide variety of publications to help you learn more about different cultures, thus enabling you to have more successful cross-cultural experiences. These include a variety of books, videotapes and simulation games that deal with topics related to intercultural communication (e.g., culture shock, living overseas, negotiation across cultures) as well as many publications that focus on specific countries and/or cultures (e.g., the Arab world, Australia, China, France, Germany, Japan, Mexico, the Philippines, Russia, Spain, Thailand, and the United States) (address at the end of Chapter 4).

Through electronic mail lists and the World Wide Web, you can learn a great deal about living and teaching in other countries. For example, there are almost daily discussions on this topic on the e-mail list, *TESLJB-L*. In addition, numerous Web sites provide information about teaching EFL in specific countries.

TOEFL (Test of English as a Foreign Language)

The TOEFL is designed to evaluate the English proficiency of people who do not speak English as a native language. Administered once a month at a number of international locations, it is required for admission by over 2,000 colleges and universities in the United States and Canada. To learn more about the test, write TOEFL Publications, P.O. Box 6161, Princeton, NJ 08541-6161, Telephone: (609) 771-7243. In addition, on the World Wide Web you can find information about TOEFL preparation, international administration sites, and dates for administration (http://www.kaplan.com/intl/toefl_top.html).

Clearinghouses and other sources of information

ERIC Clearinghouse on Languages and Linguistics/Center for Applied Linguistics offers a variety of resources for language teachers. These include two categories of free publications that deal with topics of current interest. Each is usually two pages in length. *ERIC Digests* provide summaries of research and practice (e.g., "Computer-Assisted Language Learning," "Fostering Second Language Development in Young Children"). *Minibibs* are annotated bibliographies that list approximately 12 citations of recent journal articles and documents in the ERIC database (e.g., "Developing Communicative Competence," "Second Language Learning Styles and Strategies.") ERIC also offers other publications such as research reports and a series of monographs. ERIC/CLL, 1118 22nd Street NW, Washington, DC 20037, Telephone: (202) 429-9292.

A number of overseas sources of information are available to EFL teachers. They include university sponsored clearinghouses and government subsidized centers that offer information bulletins, research findings, classroom materials, computerized information retrieval services, etc. The major centers include the following:

The British Council
10 Spring Gardens
London SW1A 2BN
United Kingdom

Centre for Information on Language Teaching and Research (CILT)
Regent's College, Inner Circle
Regent's Park
London NW1 4NS
United Kingdom

National Centre for English Language Teaching and Research (NCELTR)
Building W6C
Macquarie University
Sydney NSW 2109
Australia

Ontario Institute for Studies in Education (OISE)
252 Bloor Street West
Toronto, ON M5S 1V6
Canada

Regional English Language Centre (RELC)
30 Orange Grove Road
Singapore 1025
Republic of Singapore

References

Baurain, Bradley. April 1992. "Teaching English Feeds a Worldwide Craving." *Evangelical Missions Quarterly.* Vol. 28, No. 2, pp. 164-173.

Camenson, Blythe. 1995. *Opportunities in Teaching English to Speakers of Other Languages.* Lincolnwood, IL: NTC Publishing Group.

Crystal, David. 1987. *The Cambridge Encyclopedia of Language.* New York: Cambridge University Press.

Lakin, Paul, Ed. 1996. *The ELT Guide.* London: EFL Ltd.

Lynes, Robert. 1996. *Teaching English in Eastern and Central Europe.* Lincolnwood, IL: NTC Publishing Group.

Snow, Don. 1996. *More Than a Native Speaker: An Introduction for Volunteers Teaching Abroad.* Alexandria, VA: TESOL.

Resource Directory

The English language plays a unique role in today's global community. It is beginning to function more and more as an international language and as it does, increasing numbers of people around the world want to learn the language. Christians have been quick to recognize this need as an opportunity for service and have formed organizations to teach English both Stateside and abroad. Of course, it's not English but the gospel that most needs to be spread. For this reason, teaching is closely tied to evangelism. The organizations highlighted in the mission opportunities section are mission sending agencies that commission teachers who share the vision to serve and spread the gospel through the English classroom.

Linking service and evangelism has implications. Even if unintentional, a bad teacher is usually a bad witness. Thankfully, most organizations provide ample training for those soon to be before students. However, some may want more in-depth preparation for TEFL (Teaching English as a Foreign Language) or TESL (Teaching English as a Second Language). Teachers with advanced degrees often have more opportunities and are treated with greater respect. Further education may also be necessary for those who want to make teaching English their career ministry. The academic institutions advertising in the training opportunities section equip teachers for effective long-term service.

If you have benefitted from *The Handbook for Christian EFL Teachers,* you should be aware of other resources from the same publisher. Berry Publishing Services, Inc. is an Illinois-based publishing company committed to helping Christians make informed decisions about Christian ministry and education. BPS publications complement reader interest with options and guidance.

The Great Commission Handbook serves students and other adults who want to become more involved in missions while MISSION TODAY keeps readers up-to-date on missions around the world. For those exploring short-term missions, *The Short-Term Mission Handbook,* its companion *Leader's Guide* and *The High School Short-Term Mission Directory* are valuable resources.

Berry Publishing Services also provides annual information handbooks for those considering Christian higher education. *The Christian College Handbook* aids those exploring undergraduate institutions, and *The Seminary & Graduate School Handbook* helps those investigating Christian graduate education.

To obtain more information about the mission organizations and academic institutions featured in this directory, circle the numbers of the organizations that interest you on the "Free Information Card," or contact the organizations directly. To order copies of Berry Publishing Services publications, fill out the order card at the back of this publication or send your pre-paid order to: Distribution Manager, Berry Publishing Services, 701 Main Street, Evanston, Illinois 60202.

Mission

Teaching English as a Second Language (TESL) and Teaching English as a Foreign Language (TEFL) both have something in common when it comes to missions. They both can be used as a means of sharing the gospel in Stateside communities and in countries closed to traditional missionaries.

The following advertisements give you information on various mission agencies that commission English teachers. Note the "circle number" of the agencies that interest you. To obtain more information on these organizations, circle their corresponding number on one of the "Free Information Cards" at the back of this handbook and drop it in the mail. If you wish to make immediate contact with an agency, you can do so by calling or writing.

Opportunities

Friendship. Family. Community.

China

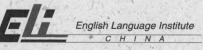

Training

An effective ministry is often rooted in the training one receives and puts into practice. In order to be a successful English teacher and bearer of the gospel's good news overseas and here-at-home, it's a good idea to start with educational preparation.

The following advertisements give you information on various academic institutions that offer English teacher training for those preparing for ministry. Note the "circle number" of the institutions that interest you. To obtain more information on these institutions, circle their corresponding number on one of the "Free Information Cards" at the back of this handbook and drop it in the mail. If you wish to make immediate contact with an institution, you can do so by calling or writing.

Opportunities

TEACH TO REACH

TESOL

- **Master of Arts in Teaching English to Speakers of Other Languages**
- **Certificate in TESOL**

Why TESOL?

- Nations around the world are demanding competent English teachers to help develop their professional labor force.
- Those holding master's degrees in TESOL are among the most sought-after professionals in the world today.
- In practice, TESOL is unparalleled in its ability to provide entry into restricted-access countries; a natural platform for cultivating cross-cultural relationships; and opportunities for initiating self-supporting educational business ventures.

Why TESOL at APU?

- Programs blend course work, practical study, and field experience.
- APU is located in the greater Los Angeles area, where more than 150 languages are spoken.
- Qualified faculty share their professional and cross-cultural experiences while adapting course work to the unique needs and interests of students.

Call **(800) TALK-APU**
or (818) 815-6000, Ext. 3844
today for more details!

AZUSA PACIFIC
U N I V E R S I T Y

Department of Global Studies and Sociology
College of Liberal Arts and Sciences
901 E. Alosta Ave., PO Box 7000, Azusa, CA 91702
http://www.apu.edu

THREE Good Reasons
to study TESL at Wheaton....

Alan Seaman
Program Coordinator
Specialist in English
for academic purposes

Cheri Pierson
Professor, Specialist in
English for biblical and
theological studies

Lonna Dickerson
Director of Institute for
Cross-Cultural Training

> **"** I appreciated the academic challenge to convert theory into practical projects which I am able to use now as a teacher of ESL. **"**
>
> Joyce Johnson, M..A. '96

THE Teaching English as a Second Language Certificate

offered at Wheaton College Graduate School will provide you with a complete program of professional preparation, including specialized areas such as literacy, curriculum and materials development, language testing, and program administration. Experienced faculty with extensive cross-cultural experience offer a dynamic synthesis of theory and practice.

DEGREE OPTIONS

You can choose to earn the TESL Certificate alone, or as part of the Master of Arts degree in Intercultural Studies. If you have earned a public school teaching certificate for Illinois, or most other states, you can add an ESL teaching endorsement by completing the TESL Certificate.

Practicum opportunities exist in over a dozen ESL programs in the Chicago area, and overseas.

Admissions Director
Wheaton College Graduate School
Wheaton, Illinois 60187-5593 • Phone: 1-800-888-0141

TESL at Carson-Newman
Bridging the Communications Gap

A Master of Arts in Teaching degree with a major in Teaching English as a Second Language (TESL) provides you with the opportunity to impact lives around the world and right here at home.

Take advantage of service and career advancement opportunities.

Acquire the tools you'll need to build bridges of opportunity to live and work abroad.

Carson-Newman's master's degree prepares you to:

- teach English in a foreign college or university
- teach English to business personnel abroad
- teach English in mission work to better communicate with those you serve

Plan for worldwide opportunities in the fields of business, education and missions...and your planning starts at Carson-Newman College.

The Department of Graduate Studies at Carson-Newman is accredited by national, regional and state agencies.

Don't be left behind. As the world gets smaller your job most likely will change to a more global-oriented outlook.

Master the possibilities with a Master of Arts in Teaching degree with a major in Teaching English as a Second Language at Carson-Newman College.

For more information, please write or call:

Jane McGill, Advisor
Graduate Admissions
and Services

Carson-Newman College
Jefferson City,
TN 37760

Call:
423-471-3460
Fax:
423-471-3475
e-mail:
graduate@cncacc.cn.edu
http://www.cn.edu

CARSON-NEWMAN COLLEGE
Jefferson City, TN 37760

At Oral Roberts University, we believe a witness of Christ is a witness of excellence.

Fulfill your calling with Excellence at ORU's Graduate School of Education and TESL Program:

- ORU's TESL Program is fully accredited, both regionally and locally.
- Practicum options include public schools, adult education, church-based programs and ORU's own English language institute-ULI.
- Financial aid and graduate assistantships available.

- The M.A. in education is a 36 hour, non-thesis program that can be completed in one year.
- Electives can be chosen from ORU's graduate schools of Business, Education or Theology/Missions.
- Instructors are experienced in ESL, with teaching experience in the U.S. and abroad.

Please contact us for more information:

Oral Roberts University
Graduate School of Education
7777 South Lewis Ave.
Tulsa, Oklahoma 74171
1-800-678-8876
Email: graded@oru.edu (grad. admissions)
or hhulling@oru.edu (TESL Coordinator)
Website: http://www.oru.edu

"God said to me, 'Raise up your students to hear My voice, to go where My light is seen dim, My voice is heard small, and My healing power is not known - even to the uttermost parts of the Earth. Their work will exceed yours and in this I am well pleased.'"

-Oral Roberts

Publications Available from Berry Publishing Services

The following pages feature available products from Berry Publishing Services, an Illinois-based publishing company that publishes books and annual information handbooks on mission, seminary/ graduate school and college opportunities. To order one or more copies of the publications listed below, fill out one of the order forms at the back of this publication and mail it with payment to: Distribution Department, Berry Publishing Services, 701 Main Street, Evanston, Illinois 60202.

Handbook for Christian EFL Teachers

With the growth of English as an international language over recent decades, Christians have realized the potential of ESL teaching as both a tentmaking and friendship evangelism tool. However, ignorance prevails about the available opportunities and issues involved in teaching English as a Foreign Language (TEFL). The *Handbook for Christian EFL Teachers* is an anecdote to such inadequacy, providing a prospective teacher with a wealth of resources for making informed decisions about training options, teaching opportunities, and instructional materials.

The *Handbook* gives readers direction for setting goals and making decisions. It offers a comprehensive overview of the choices one needs to make when considering a TEFL ministry. It demonstrates the expectations mission agencies and other organizations have for teachers and describe the training necessary for participation their programs. The *Handbook for Christian EFL Teachers* presents a balanced discussion of the advantages of different options in the TEFL ministry.

PRICES:
A single copy is $8; 5+ copies are $7 each; 10+ copies are $6 each; 25+ copies are $5 each.

TO ORDER:
Fill out the order card at the back of this publication. Or, send your pre-paid order to: Distribution Manager, Berry Publishing Services, 701 Main Street, Evanston, Illinois, 60202.

Teaching More Than English: Using TESL/TEFL on the Mission Field at Home and Abroad

Many people wonder how their teaching gift can be used in missions. This book can help them find the answer. *Teaching More Than English* is a unique publication containing inspiring stories written by people who are teaching English both here-at-home and overseas through which they share wisdom and principles gained from personal experience.

The informative how-to articles help the readers set themselves on the path to teaching. The resource directory offers possibilities for TEFL training programs and mission opportunities. This one-of-a-kind volume serves as a resource for those interested in using TESL/TEFL as means toward sharing the gospel. *Teaching More Than English* is also an ideal resource for the student, layperson or missionary/church staff already involved with TEFL (Teaching English as a Foreign Language) or TESL (Teaching English as a Second Language).

PRICES:
A single copy is $8; 5+ copies are $7 each; 10+ copies are $6 each; 25+ copies are $5 each.

TO ORDER:
Fill out the order card at the back of this publication. Or, send your pre-paid order to: Distribution Manager, Berry Publishing Services, 701 Main Street, Evanston, Illinois, 60202.

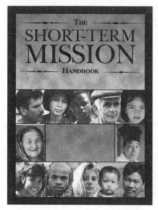

The Short-Term Mission Handbook

Short-term missions are taking place throughout the world, providing a window to missions for many Christians. *The Short-Term Mission Handbook* is an important resource for anyone considering short-term missions. It guides you through the missions experience—from planning a trip to actually going on one. Every leader and team participant will be informed and motivated by the editorial features and how-to articles. This "A to Z" resource is packed with articles by key Christian leaders involved in short-term ministries.

Featured articles range broadly in topic. These will answer questions readers may have regarding missions, as well as help resolve problems that may arise during the ministry encounter. Some articles describe specific skills readers can use on trips, such as medicine, music and sports. Other articles give practical tips on issues of fund-raising, pre-field training, developing team spirit, cultural consideration and more. *The Short-Term Mission Handbook* also provides a wide range of mission sending organizations for readers to contact, helping them find the place God has for them.

PRICES:
A single copy is $8; 5+ copies are $7 each; 10+ copies are $6 each; 25+ copies are $5 each.

TO ORDER:
Fill out the order card at the back of this publication. Or, send your pre-paid order to: Distribution Manager, Berry Publishing Services, 701 Main Street, Evanston, Illinois, 60202.

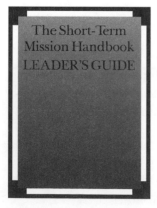

The Short-Term Mission Handbook — Leader's Guide

The companion to *The Short-Term Mission Handbook* is designed to help team leaders prepare for their short-term experience and make it a success. The *Leader's Guide* complements *The Short-Term Mission Handbook* by providing additional in-depth information just for team leaders.

To assist leaders in planning for their short-term mission experience, the *Leader's Guide* presents articles, charts and worksheets as a curriculum supplement. Articles contribute personal experiences, charts present ministry opportunities and worksheets guide leaders through the various components of a missions experience. Profile articles describing mission organizations, training institutions and resources give readers an informational base from which to draw.

PRICES:
A single copy is $12; 5+ copies are $10 each; 10+ copies are $8 each; 25+ copies are $6 each.

TO ORDER:
Fill out the order card at the back of this publication. Or, send your pre-paid order to: Distribution Manager, Berry Publishing Services, 701 Main Street, Evanston, Illinois, 60202.

Charting Your Journey to the Nations

This interactive workbook co-authored by William D. Taylor (WEF Missions Commission) and Steve Hoke (Church Resource Ministries) promises to become an indispensable tool in recruiting North Americans for the cause of world missions. *Charting Your Journey to the Nations* is the official replacement for the much-loved, long-used and now out-of-print *You Can So Get There From Here* (first published by MARC in 1969).

The three major sections—getting ready, getting there and getting established—take the workbook user from initial interest in missions to life and ministry on the field. Readers will ask themselves probing questions and decide what their involvement with missions will be as they work through this book.

Charting Your Journey to the Nations contains a special resource directory to serve as a means for choosing missions organizations, selected educational institutions and information providers (publishers, travel companies, missions resources) to equip you for ministry.

PRICES:
A single copy is $8; 5+ copies are $7 each; 10+ copies are $6 each; 25+ copies are $5 each.

TO ORDER:
Fill out the order card at the back of this publication. Or, send your pre-paid order to: Distribution Manager, Berry Publishing Services, 701 Main Street, Evanston, Illinois, 60202.

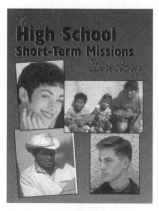

The High School Short-Term Missions Directory

Listing virtually every missions opportunity available to Christian young people—overseas options across the globe, domestic opportunities and service projects—*The High School Short-Term Missions Directory* is a must for every Christian teenager considering short-term missions involvement.

This directory aims to inform students of possibilities and supply the practical means to getting connected with the right programs. Organizations provide basic information: a description their missions focus, requirements, dates of programs, types of projects available, training, staff, and more. Listings of addresses, phone numbers, and names of contacts provide a vital link for students to gain further information about the opportunities that interest them. The amount of information consolidated and made easily accessible makes this directory a valuable resource for teenagers exploring avenues for missions involvement.

PRICE:
$8/copy

TO ORDER:
Fill out the order card at the back of this publication. Or, send your pre-paid order to: Distribution Manager, Berry Publishing Services, 701 Main Street, Evanston, Illinois, 60202.

Mission Today

Reading *Mission Today* is one way to stay current on mission topics and the spread of the gospel worldwide. The lengthy annual edition brings you the most comprehensive overview of missions across the globe and here in North America.

To serve its thoughtful, mission-minded audience, *Mission Today* seeks both breadth and depth in its coverage. It exposes the reader to the many varieties of ministry, such as children's ministry, medical missions, relief and development, Bible translation, or Native American ministry. It reports on how the gospel is spreading in specific regions of the world and highlights the particular problems and issues different areas face, from unreached peoples of South America to the urban youths of Chicago. It balances the theoretical and the practical, discussing issues such as current trends and strategies in missions while also offering advice on fund raising or training for ministry. Those who think and care deeply about missions in the contemporary world will find *Mission Today* an invaluable resource.

PRICES:
A single-copy mailed 1st class is $5; 3+ copies are $3 each; 15+ copies are $2 each.

TO ORDER:
Fill out the order card at the back of this publication. Or, send your pre-paid order to: Distribution Manager, Berry Publishing Services, 701 Main Street, Evanston, Illinois, 60202.

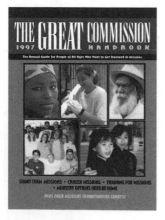

The Great Commission Handbook

The Great Commission Handbook is the annual guide for those who want to become involved in missions. It seeks to answer the question, "Where do I begin?" through articles covering the most important issues and mission opportunities. Ideal for adults and students alike, *The Great Commission Handbook* is an effective resource to pass out to missions classes, Sunday School groups and missions conference attendees.

Each issue is designed to take a reader's interest in missions and nourish it with articles that are both practical and conceptual. It guides readers as they begin thinking about experiencing missions first-hand and explains the rationale for mission involvement.

A short-term missions section outlines ways to take concrete steps toward gaining valuable missions experiences. Articles on career missions explore long-term avenues for ministry, with topics ranging from practical advice to specific examples and issues to consider in thinking about missions. A final "section deals with how to be equipped for effective missions involvement, describing the importance of training and what the options are for preparation. The combination of how-to articles, insightful features, personal accounts and valuable, informational charts results in a handbook useful to anyone taking their first steps toward missions.

PRICES:

A single-copy mailed 1st class is $5; 3+ copies are $3 each; 15+ copies are $2 each.

TO ORDER:

Fill out the order card at the back of this publication. Or, send your pre-paid order to:
Distribution Manager, Berry Publishing Services, 701 Main Street, Evanston, Illinois, 60202.

The Seminary & Graduate School Handbook

The Seminary & Graduate School Handbook is devoted to reaching potential students with information on seminaries, Christian graduate schools, alternative non-graduate programs and external studies programs. Articles, charts, informational listings and other features assist readers in choosing the options best for them.

It is the only publication of its kind and it takes promoting Christian graduate education seriously. For this reason, *The Seminary & Graduate School Handbook* aims to expose readers not just to the facts and figures of schools but also to the broader concepts and issues involved. Feature articles address the nature of seminary education, trends in graduate education and issues in evangelical scholarship and ministry training.

The Seminary & Graduate School Handbook regularly includes authors who are not just writing about seminary but who are actually involved in shaping what evangelical education is today. It also explores the full range of educational possibilities, including traditional seminary degrees, new graduate programs in business and opportunities on the Internet.

PRICES:

A single-copy mailed 1st class is $5; 3+ copies are $3 each; 15+ copies are $2 each.

TO ORDER:

Fill out the order card at the back of this publication. Or, send your pre-paid order to:
Distribution Manager, Berry Publishing Services, 701 Main Street, Evanston, Illinois, 60202.

Continued ➤

The Christian College Handbook

Containing up-to-date information on more than 200 of the best Christian liberal arts colleges and Bible colleges, *The Christian College Handbook* is the most comprehensive resource published anywhere on locating the Christian college that's right for you.

The Christian College Handbook assumes that choosing a college is among the most important choices in life. For this reason, it provides resources for all aspects of the decision process, from visiting colleges to financial aid. Since decisions require imagining what the future might be like, *The Christian College Handbook* offers articles on college life, such as choosing a major and getting along with your roommate. Charts of majors, campus facts and figures help determine how schools measure up to each other. Articles discuss the uniqueness of Christian colleges and encourage teenagers to think through why they might attend a Christian school and to have clear reasons for their decision.

PRICES:
A single-copy mailed 1st class is $5; 3+ copies are $3 each; 15+ copies are $2 each.

TO ORDER:
Fill out the order card at the back of this publication. Or, send your pre-paid order to: Distribution Manager, Berry Publishing Services, 701 Main Street, Evanston, Illinois, 60202.

How to Order
Publications from
Berry Publishing Services

To order Berry Publishing Services publications featured in this resource section, fill out the order card at the back of this publication. Or, fill out the order form below and mail it to: Distribution Manager, Berry Publishing Services, 701 Main Street, Evanston, Illinois 60202. Or, fax your order to (847) 869-6921.

* *

❑ **YES!** Please send the publication(s) I have requested below. I have enclosed payment with this order and understand that my order will be filled promptly.

* *

The following are available: 1-4 copies are $8 each; 5+ copies are $7 each; 10+ copies are $6 each; 25+ copies are $5 each.

_____ copies of the *Handbook for Christian EFL Teachers* at $_____ per copy = $_____.

_____ copies of *Teaching More Than English* at $_____ per copy = $_____.

_____ copies of *The Short-Term Mission Handbook* at $_____ per copy = $_____.

_____ copies of *The High School Short-Term Mission Directory* at $_____ per copy = $_____.

_____ copies of *Charting Your Journey to the Nations* at $_____ per copy = $_____.

The following are available for $1/copy provided you order one or more copies of the above publications. Otherwise, a single-copy mailed 1st class is $5; 3+ copies are $2 each, 15+ copies are $1 each.

_____ copies of *The Great Commission Handbook* at $_____ copy = $_____.

_____ copies of *MISSION TODAY* at $_____ copy = $_____.

_____ copies of *The Seminary & Graduate School Handbook* at $_____ copy = $_____.

_____ copies of *The Christian College Handbook* at $_____ copy = $_____.

— OVER →

A companion *Leader's Guide* to *The Short-Term Mission Handbook* is available: 1-4 copies are $12 each; 5+ copies are $10 each; 10+ copies are $8 each; 25+ copies are $6 each.

_____ copies of the *Leader's Guide* at $_____ copy = $_____.

Total amount enclosed $_____.

Send to:

_____
Name   Title

_____
Address

_____
City   State   Zip

_____
Telephone

_____
Organization/Church/School Name

FREE INFO !

To obtain additional information from any advertiser listed below, print your name and address to the left, circle the numbers of the advertisers of interest to you and drop this postage-paid card in the mail.

PLEASE PRINT

First Name _____ Last Name _____

Address _____

City _____ State _____ Zip _____

Telephone _____

Age:
A☐ Under 20   B☐ 20-30
C☐ 31-40   D☐ 41-50
E☐ 51-65   F☐ Over 65

The information I request is for:
1☐ Immediate Use
2☐ Future Use
3☐ Reference Use

Please check one:
A☐ Mission-Minded Adult
B☐ Pastor/Mission Pastor
C☐ Missions Committee Member
D☐ Church Leader
E☐ Retired Adult
F☐ Working Adult
G☐ High School Student
H☐ College Student
I☐ Graduate or Seminary Student

Arab World Ministries . . . . p. 76 (#001)
Azusa Pacific University . . . . . . p. 81 (#002)
Biola University . . . . pp. 80, 82 (#003)
Campus Crusade for Christ . . . . . p. 78 (#004)
Carson-Newman College . . . . . . p. 85 (#005)
China Educational Exchange . . . . p. 77 (#006)
China Harvest . . . . p. 78 (#007)
Christian Advance International . . . . pp. 74, 77 (#008)
Columbia International University . . . . p. 83 (#009)
Educational Resources and Referrals/China . . . . p. 77 (#010)
Educational Services International . . . . p. 77 (#011)
English Language Institute/China . . . . p. 79 (#012)
Goshen College . . . . p. 83 (#013)
Institute for Cross-Cultural Training . . . . . pp. 82, 86 (#014)

International Messengers . . . . p. 83 (#028)
InterServe . . . . p. 78 (#015)
Japan English Centers Ministry . . . . p. 77 (#016)
Mennonite Central Committee . . . p. 75 (#017)
Mission Society for United Methodists . . . . p. 76 (#018)
Mission to Unreached Peoples . . p. 76 (#019)
NICS . . . . p. 75 (#020)
OMF International . . . . p. 78 (#021)
OMS International . . . . p. 74 (#022)
Oral Roberts University . . . . p. 87 (#023)
Russian American Christian University . . . . p. 75 (#025)
Seattle Pacific University . . . . . . p. 80 (#024)
TEAM . . . . p. 76
Toccoa Falls College . . . . p. 83 (#026)
Wheaton College Graduate School . . . . p. 84 (#027)

Expires July, 2000   TEFL 96

FREE INFO !

To obtain additional information from any advertiser listed below, print your name and address to the left, circle the numbers of the advertisers of interest to you and drop this postage-paid card in the mail.

PLEASE PRINT

First Name _____ Last Name _____

Address _____

City _____ State _____ Zip _____

Telephone _____

Age:
A☐ Under 20   B☐ 20-30
C☐ 31-40   D☐ 41-50
E☐ 51-65   F☐ Over 65

The information I request is for:
1☐ Immediate Use
2☐ Future Use
3☐ Reference Use

Please check one:
A☐ Mission-Minded Adult
B☐ Pastor/Mission Pastor
C☐ Missions Committee Member
D☐ Church Leader
E☐ Retired Adult
F☐ Working Adult
G☐ High School Student
H☐ College Student
I☐ Graduate or Seminary Student

Arab World Ministries . . . . p. 76 (#001)
Azusa Pacific University . . . . . . p. 81 (#002)
Biola University . . . . pp. 80, 82 (#003)
Campus Crusade for Christ . . . . . p. 78 (#004)
Carson-Newman College . . . . . . p. 85 (#005)
China Educational Exchange . . . . p. 77 (#006)
China Harvest . . . . p. 78 (#007)
Christian Advance International . . . . pp. 74, 77 (#008)
Columbia International University . . . . p. 83 (#009)
Educational Resources and Referrals/China . . . . p. 77 (#010)
Educational Services International . . . . p. 77 (#011)
English Language Institute/China . . . . p. 79 (#012)
Goshen College . . . . p. 83 (#013)
Institute for Cross-Cultural Training . . . . . pp. 82, 86 (#014)

International Messengers . . . . p. 83 (#028)
InterServe . . . . p. 78 (#015)
Japan English Centers Ministry . . . . p. 77 (#016)
Mennonite Central Committee . . . p. 75 (#017)
Mission Society for United Methodists . . . . p. 76 (#018)
Mission to Unreached Peoples . . p. 76 (#019)
NICS . . . . p. 75 (#020)
OMF International . . . . p. 78 (#021)
OMS International . . . . p. 74 (#022)
Oral Roberts University . . . . p. 87 (#023)
Russian American Christian University . . . . p. 75 (#025)
Seattle Pacific University . . . . . . p. 80 (#024)
TEAM . . . . p. 76
Toccoa Falls College . . . . p. 83 (#026)
Wheaton College Graduate School . . . . p. 84 (#027)

Expires July, 2000   TEFL 96

BUSINESS REPLY MAIL
FIRST CLASS   PERMIT NO. 293   EVANSTON, IL

POSTAGE WILL BE PAID BY ADDRESSEE

NO POSTAGE
NECESSARY
IF MAILED
IN THE
UNITED STATES

BERRY PUBLISHING SERVICES, INC.
701 MAIN ST.
EVANSTON, IL 60202-9908

BUSINESS REPLY MAIL
FIRST CLASS   PERMIT NO. 293   EVANSTON, IL

POSTAGE WILL BE PAID BY ADDRESSEE

NO POSTAGE
NECESSARY
IF MAILED
IN THE
UNITED STATES

BERRY PUBLISHING SERVICES, INC.
701 MAIN ST.
EVANSTON, IL 60202-9908

BUSINESS REPLY MAIL
FIRST CLASS   PERMIT NO. 293   EVANSTON, IL

POSTAGE WILL BE PAID BY ADDRESSEE

NO POSTAGE
NECESSARY
IF MAILED
IN THE
UNITED STATES

BERRY PUBLISHING SERVICES, INC.
701 MAIN ST.
EVANSTON, IL 60202-9908

ORDER FORM

To order any of the publications featured in this handbook book, fill out both sides of this order form and mail it with your payment to: Distribution Manager, Berry Publishing Services, 701 Main Street, Evanston, Illinois 60202

❏ **YES!** Please send the publication(s) I have requested below. I have enclosed payment with this order and understand that my order will be filled promptly.

The following publications are available for $8/copy; 5+ copies are $7 each; 10+ copies are $6 each; 25+ copies are $5 each.

_____ copies of the *Handbook for Christian EFL Teachers* at $_____/copy = $_____.

_____ copies of *Teaching More Than English* at $_____/copy = $_____.

_____ copies of *The Short-Term Mission Handbook* at $_____/copy = $_____.

_____ copies of *The High School Short-Term Mission Directory* at $_____/copy = $_____.

_____ copies of *Charting Your Journey to the Nations* at $_____/copy = $_____.

The following publications are available for $1/copy provided you order one or more copies of the above publications. Otherwise, a single-copy mailed 1st class is $5; 3+ copies are $2 each, 15+ copies are $1 each.

_____ copies of *The Great Commission Handbook* at $_____/copy = $_____.

— OVER —

TEFL 96

ORDER FORM

To order any of the publications featured in this handbook book, fill out both sides of this order form and mail it with your payment to: Distribution Manager, Berry Publishing Services, 701 Main Street, Evanston, Illinois 60202

❏ **YES!** Please send the publication(s) I have requested below. I have enclosed payment with this order and understand that my order will be filled promptly.

The following publications are available for $8/copy; 5+ copies are $7 each; 10+ copies are $6 each; 25+ copies are $5 each.

_____ copies of the *Handbook for Christian EFL Teachers* at $_____/copy = $_____.

_____ copies of *Teaching More Than English* at $_____/copy = $_____.

_____ copies of *The Short-Term Mission Handbook* at $_____/copy = $_____.

_____ copies of *The High School Short-Term Mission Directory* at $_____/copy = $_____.

_____ copies of *Charting Your Journey to the Nations* at $_____/copy = $_____.

The following publications are available for $1/copy provided you order one or more copies of the above publications. Otherwise, a single-copy mailed 1st class is $5; 3+ copies are $2 each, 15+ copies are $1 each.

_____ copies of *The Great Commission Handbook* at $_____/copy = $_____.

— OVER —

TEFL 96

ORDER FORM

To order any of the publications featured in this handbook book, fill out both sides of this order form and mail it with your payment to: Distribution Manager, Berry Publishing Services, 701 Main Street, Evanston, Illinois 60202

❏ **YES!** Please send the publication(s) I have requested below. I have enclosed payment with this order and understand that my order will be filled promptly.

The following publications are available for $8/copy; 5+ copies are $7 each; 10+ copies are $6 each; 25+ copies are $5 each.

_____ copies of the *Handbook for Christian EFL Teachers* at $_____/copy = $_____.

_____ copies of *Teaching More Than English* at $_____/copy = $_____.

_____ copies of *The Short-Term Mission Handbook* at $_____/copy = $_____.

_____ copies of *The High School Short-Term Mission Directory* at $_____/copy = $_____.

_____ copies of *Charting Your Journey to the Nations* at $_____/copy = $_____.

The following publications are available for $1/copy provided you order one or more copies of the above publications. Otherwise, a single-copy mailed 1st class is $5; 3+ copies are $2 each, 15+ copies are $1 each.

_____ copies of *The Great Commission Handbook* at $_____/copy = $_____.

— OVER —

TEFL 96

ORDER FORM

To order any of the publications featured in this handbook book, fill out both sides of this order form and mail it with your payment to: Distribution Manager, Berry Publishing Services, 701 Main Street, Evanston, Illinois 60202

_____ copies of *Mission Today*
    at $_____/copy = $_____.

_____ copies of *The Seminary & Graduate School Handbook*
    at $_____/copy = $_____.

_____ copies of *The Christian College Handbook*
    at $_____/copy = $_____.

A companion *Leader's Guide* to *The Short-Term Mission Handbook* is available for $12/copy; 5+ copies are $10 each; 10+ copies are $8 each; 25+ copies are $6 each.

_____ copies of *Leader's Guide*
    at $_____/copy = $_____.

Total amount enclosed $_____.

PLEASE PRINT

First Name   Last Name   Title   City   State   Zip

Address   Telephone   Organization/Church/School Name

TEFL 96

ORDER FORM

To order any of the publications featured in this handbook book, fill out both sides of this order form and mail it with your payment to: Distribution Manager, Berry Publishing Services, 701 Main Street, Evanston, Illinois 60202

_____ copies of *Mission Today*
    at $_____/copy = $_____.

_____ copies of *The Seminary & Graduate School Handbook*
    at $_____/copy = $_____.

_____ copies of *The Christian College Handbook*
    at $_____/copy = $_____.

A companion *Leader's Guide* to *The Short-Term Mission Handbook* is available for $12/copy; 5+ copies are $10 each; 10+ copies are $8 each; 25+ copies are $6 each.

_____ copies of *Leader's Guide*
    at $_____/copy = $_____.

Total amount enclosed $_____.

PLEASE PRINT

First Name   Last Name   Title   City   State   Zip

Address   Telephone   Organization/Church/School Name

TEFL 96

ORDER FORM

To order any of the publications featured in this handbook book, fill out both sides of this order form and mail it with your payment to: Distribution Manager, Berry Publishing Services, 701 Main Street, Evanston, Illinois 60202

_____ copies of *Mission Today*
    at $_____/copy = $_____.

_____ copies of *The Seminary & Graduate School Handbook*
    at $_____/copy = $_____.

_____ copies of *The Christian College Handbook*
    at $_____/copy = $_____.

A companion *Leader's Guide* to *The Short-Term Mission Handbook* is available for $12/copy; 5+ copies are $10 each; 10+ copies are $8 each; 25+ copies are $6 each.

_____ copies of *Leader's Guide*
    at $_____/copy = $_____.

Total amount enclosed $_____.

PLEASE PRINT

First Name   Last Name   Title   City   State   Zip

Address   Telephone   Organization/Church/School Name

TEFL 96